THE LONG WAY HOME
REVISED EDITION

A Journey Into History With Captain Robert Ford

By

Ed Dover

Library of Congress Catalog Registration Number: TXu 1-577-228
Dated May 27, 2008.
Cataloged as:
Ed Dover
The Long Way Home – Revised Edition

All black and white photos of B314 aircraft and crew members courtesy of Pan Am Historical Foundation and obtained from the Pan Am Historical Foundation CD "Pan Am 1927-1991 The Story in Pictures". For more information go to www.panam.org.

ISBN 978-0-615-21472-6

TABLE OF CONTENTS

DEDICATION

This work is dedicated to Captain Robert Ford, a true Master of Ocean Flying Boats and a legend in his own time.

FOREWORD

Robert Ford was born in Cambridge, Massachusetts, in 1906. The son of a renowned Harvard University scholar, he went to public schools, attended Harvard, studied for a year at the Sorbonne, and returned to Harvard in 1926. After graduating in his father's field, Romance Languages, he returned to Harvard and attended engineering school, intending to become an aviator.

Ford went to Navy flight school at Pensacola, Florida, obtained his wings, and joined the Fleet as an aviator. He was assigned to the Scouting Force, Atlantic Fleet, on the old *Arkansas*. This was in the biplane days, and the scout planes were seaplanes. They were flung off the ship by a gunpowder-driven catapult atop the after main gun mount. On return from scouting, assuming they could locate the ship, they landed alongside it on the water. Finally, they were hoisted aboard with a crane. Ford enjoyed his hitch as an Ensign, put in a lot of flight time, and made many friends. He realized, however, that there was no future in the U. S. Navy for a non-Academy man, and left the Navy after one tour.

The Great Depression was well under way when Ford left the Navy. He went home to Cambridge, and began working relentlessly at the task of finding a flying job with an airline. Andre Priester, who was establishing Pan American World Airways, agreed to take him on in 1934. Priester was convinced that a strong safety record was essential to operating a successful airline, and that training was the way to be safe. In addition to flying, potential Pan American pilots became specialists in airframe and engine mechanics, radio operation, navigation, and weather forecasting.

1

Ford progressed through the Pan American training, and flew Curtis Commodores and Sikorsky S-40s down the Atlantic seaboard into South America. By the start of World War II, Ford was a Captain in the larger and longer-ranged Boeing B-314 flying boats. In 1940 he was transferred to the Pacific Division flying from San Francisco to Hawaii and the South Pacific.

In 1934, as soon as he started the Pan American job, Ford married Elizabeth Evans, daughter of a successful New York businessman. Together they had an affectionate marriage that spanned almost sixty years. They had four children between 1939 and 1949, three boys and a girl, two of whom were born before his transfer to the Pacific.

Michael Ford
February, 1998

ACKNOWLEDGMENTS

I would like to express my grateful thanks to all those who contributed to the completion of this work; especially to the late Captain Robert Ford and his wife Betty, for their warmth and hospitality in allowing me to invade their lives, while they were still with us, in pursuit of this story. I thank also, their son Michael Ford, for contributing the biographical foreword describing his father's early years, and for his pilot's expertise in clarifying some of the technical aspects of operating high-powered aircraft; and the late Flight Radio Officer Eugene Leach, for his valuable help in the final months of the project.

Although we did not have a chance to meet, I would like to thank the late John D. Steers, Fourth Officer, whose written log, passed along to me by both Captain Ford and Eugene Leach, provided a wealth of detail that helped fan the fires of creative imagination as I participated vicariously in the amazing adventure that was the flight of Clipper NC18602.

My thanks also to the late Betty Ford, Mary Steers, and Marian Rothe for their help and cooperation in providing me with some of the personal details of their husbands' lives following the completion of the flight.

Thanks to Barbara Beery and her sister Katherine "Kitty" Tilleman for providing post-flight information about their father, Flight Radio Officer Oscar Hendrickson regarding his assignments and career following the flight.

3

I am indebted to both the old Pan American Airways and the Boeing Aircraft Company for providing photographs and technical data which I used in a 1968 article about the Boeing Clippers and which served as a valuable reference during the writing of this book.

Special thanks to Mr. Douglas Miller, of Pelican Films, for his timely contribution of the copy of the Cairo letter which he provided in time to be included in the book. The contents and significance of the letter are discussed in the Appendix.

A big thank-you to Mr. Derek R. Hughey of Tacoma, Washington for his contribution of copies of First Officer John Mack's pilot flight log and an article from the *Vacaville Reporter VISTA Magazine* of January 1972 featuring an interview with First Officer Mack on the occasion of his retirement from Pan American.

To Mrs. Merry Herd Barton, who, as a five year old child, was one of the evacuees from Noumea to Gladstone, grateful thanks for her information about her father, Folger Athearn, the Pan American station manager at Noumea at that time.

AUTHOR'S PREFACE

Following the Japanese attack on Pearl Harbor on December 7, 1941, a giant four-engine Pan American Airways Boeing flying boat, registered as NC18602, under the command of Captain Robert Ford, embarked on a remarkable journey. Caught en route over the South Pacific at the time of the Japanese attack, Captain Ford and his crew were forced into a flight plan than none of them had anticipated when they left San Francisco on December 1st for what was to have been a routine round trip commercial flight to Auckland, New Zealand. Faced with the threat of interception by Japanese forces, they were ordered to take their strategically valuable aircraft on a globe-girdling, 31,500 mile, six-week odyssey, heading westward mostly across territory that had never been flown over before by such a large commercial aircraft. With no suitable navigation charts, no certainty of obtaining fuel or servicing, and under a total veil of secrecy and radio blackout, they threaded their way across the war zones of the Far East, the Middle East, Africa, the South Atlantic, Brazil, and the Caribbean, to bring their aircraft home safely to New York. This is the story of that historic flight as related to me in person by Captain Robert Ford.

In January, 1992, I visited Captain Ford at his ranch in Northern California. I spent two days as his guest and obtained almost three hours of taped interviews. He also gave me a copy of the flight log kept by Fourth Officer John D. Steers.

In August, 1993, I visited with Eugene Leach, the radio operator who came on board at Noumea. He also gave me additional photo-copies of John Steer's flight log.

During the early phases of my research one unresolved question remained: was there one aircraft or two involved in the flight? Later research has confirmed that Ford used another B-314 for the flight legs from San Francisco to San Pedro to Honolulu. According to Fourth Officer John Steers' flight log the other aircraft was NC18606. They picked up NC18602 at Honolulu for the flight south.

Another interesting fact is that First Officer John Mack was not with Ford on the flight legs from San Francisco to San Pedro to Honolulu. Mack had called in to say that he could not make the flight in time to depart with Ford. Pan Am operations hurriedly enlisted the services of another First Officer – Thomas N. White, Sr – to take Mack's place. This situation is described more fully in Chapter One. The quoted dialogue is my best attempt to reflect what might have been said at any given time during the flight. Some of it is based on the personal statements of Bob Ford, much of it on my own experience as a Pan American Flight Radio Officer on board other B-314 flying boats. To the best of my knowledge no verbatim record was ever kept of the exact conversations that took place during the course of the flight. In some cases, where it was not possible to obtain exact details, I have used fictional names for some of the ground personnel they met along the way.

The quoted contents of the Plan A letter and the telegrams that Ford received at Auckland are also my own interpretations of what they contained based upon my interviews with Captain Ford. Most of these records have been lost after the passage of more than 66 years. But the details of the flight, the identities of the flight crew and the events which occurred: all these are true.

Ed Dover
Albuquerque, New Mexico
May, 2007

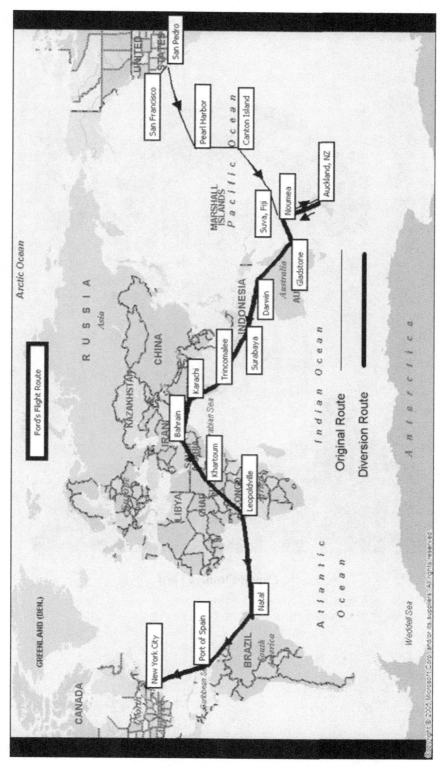

7

Captain Robert Ford

**NC18602 on its docking cradle at Treasure Island in San Francisco Bay
(Boeing Aircraft Photo).**

CHAPTER I

FOR CAPTAIN'S EYES ONLY

Captain Robert Ford scanned the sky over San Francisco Bay on December 1, 1941 as he walked – almost marched – in Pan American style military formation with his flight crew down the Treasure Island ramp toward the big flying boat. He pulled his jacket tighter against the chill of the breeze coming across the water. As he approached the gangway leading from the dock to the sea wing entrance of the flying boat he scanned the underside of the engine nacelles looking for any tell-tale sign of oil seepage that might require investigation. He also inspected the trailing edges of the wing and stabilizer looking for anything that might be amiss with the control surfaces.

Ford was a veteran pilot for Pan American; spare and wiry with what could only be described as "pilot's eyes" – keen and bright with just a touch of crow's feet at the corners. Years of squinting into distant horizons, as he flew the early flying boats over Pan American's oceanic air routes, had left their mark on his deeply tanned face. Whenever he came aboard one of the big Clippers he brought a commanding presence onto the flight deck. From his earliest days as a Navy pilot Ford had been a natural airman. Every long-time Pan American pilot of his era could attest to the rigid drill required to advance from Fourth Officer through Third, Second and First Officer ranks. Then, if he survived that long, he faced the final challenge of qualifying as a "Master of Ocean Flying Boats"; a majestically sonorous title that was all the more impressive considering the technical stature and performance of the flying machine that had to be mastered to achieve that rank.

In the late 1930s and early 1940s a Pan American Airways Model 314 Boeing Clipper was awesome to watch as it sat on the water, rocking placidly at its mooring at Treasure Island in San Francisco Bay: a huge streamlined hull, 106 feet long; the great tapered wing spanning 152 feet from tip to tip. Even though it weighed 82,500 pounds it seemed to float lightly on the water.

B314 Main Lounge and Dining Salon (Boeing Aircraft photo).

B314 plush, comfortable seating for all passengers (Pan American Airways photo).

The compartmented passenger section had a daytime seating capacity of 74 and a nighttime sleeping capacity of 34 to 40. The spacious dining salon could seat 14 people at a time, as white-coated stewards served formal meals, complete with fine table linen, china and silverware. A spiral staircase led to the flight deck "upstairs" where the Captain commanded and directed his crew in all aspects of the ship's operations. From this deck each crew member exercised his particular specialized talents in the process of carrying well-pampered passengers across the oceans to destinations that most ordinary people could only dream about. Since the Sikorsky S-40 of 1931 all Pan American flying boats, including the famous Martin M-130 *China Clipper*, had been named like the famous sailing ships of the previous century, But the Boeing was the biggest and best of them all.

The Captain and First Officer did the primary piloting. The Captain was always at the controls for landings and takeoffs. The Second Officer was primarily responsible for navigation. The Third

Officer acted as relief pilot for the Second Officer and, while on the water, was responsible for handling and mooring. The Fourth Officer acted as general pilot relief for the other four pilots in both ground and flight duties.

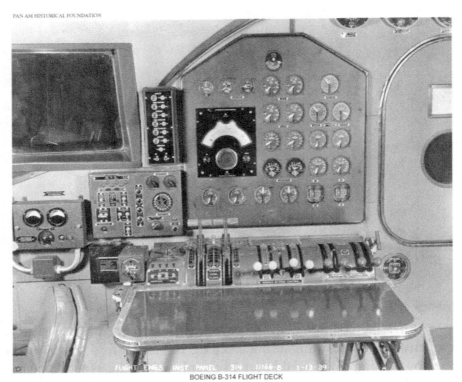

BOEING B-314 FLIGHT DECK

Engineer's Station on the B-314

Two engineering officers managed the four Wright GR-2600-A2 power plants. Each engine was capable of generating 1,600 horsepower for takeoff. The aircraft's wing was so thick along the leading edge that internal catwalks were installed there, allowing the crew access to each engine compartment during flight.

Two radio officers took shifts in manning the radio desk from which they kept in touch with Pan Am's bases while over the oceans. Morse Code was the over-ocean communications medium of choice at a time when voice communications was limited to within a few miles of each landing terminal.

Below, in the passenger cabin, two white-coated stewards managed the galley and saw to the passengers' creature comforts.

Ford walked down the gangway followed by his crew. Also accompanying him was Jack Poindexter, Chief Flight Radio Officer for Pan Am's Pacific Division. Poindexter looked up at the radio antenna wires strung between the vertical stabilizers and the fuselage. As with all of Pan Am's Flight Radio Officers, he knew the importance of checking all parts of the aircraft's radio equipment to ensure that they were in good working order before any flight; and this included a thorough pre-flight inspection of the antennas. He was especially aware of that concern now because he was checking out new radio equipment that had recently been installed aboard the B-314s. This short flight, from San Francisco to the Los Angeles flying boat station at San Pedro, would give him a chance to put that equipment through its paces before the Clipper set out on its scheduled run to Honolulu.

They crossed the sea wing and entered the cabin. Ground service personnel were busy moving through the passenger area loading provisions and getting ready to receive passengers. Ford, his crew and Poindexter moved forward to the spiral stairway that led up to the flight deck. As they emerged from the stairwell each crew member went to his assigned station to begin pre-flight checks. Oscar Hendrickson, First Radio Officer, went to the radio desk and began checking the receivers. Poindexter stood beside him to observe his procedures. "How do the new receivers look to you, Oscar?"

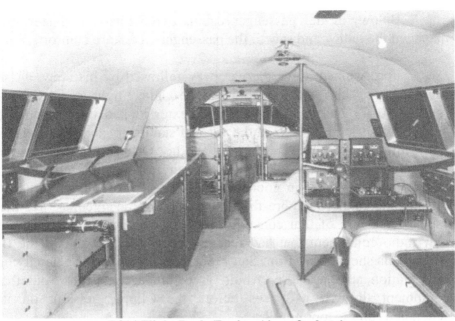

B314 Flight Deck (Boeing Aircraft photo).

B314 Cockpit and Instrument Panel (Boeing Aircraft photo).

"So far, so good. Just checking the DF function right now. That new A and N homing receiver looks pretty good. Anything special we need to know about it before we go?"

"No, just what we covered in the class briefing. Main thing is the sharpness of the on-course signal, but we won't be able to check that until we're airborne. Where's your assistant?"

"That would be Harry Strickland. He's waiting for us at San Pedro. We'll be picking him up down there. You coming to Honolulu with us?"

"No. Just as far as San Pedro. The front office asked me to ride shotgun on these new receivers and transmitters just far enough to make sure they're okay for the long haul. I don't imagine we'll have any problems with 'em but they wanted me to check 'em out, just to be sure. But I wish they'd given me notice on it sooner. Looks like I'll have to take a late flight back from L.A. I've already phoned my wife to hold supper for me."

"That's what you get for being the Chief and not one of the Indians!" Hendrickson quipped, grinning at his boss.

"Is that the new equipment they showed us in the demo meeting yesterday?" Bob Ford asked Poindexter.

"Yeah...just installed this morning."

"They gave us just a quick peek. That A and N homer sounds interesting. Think we can get a good checkout on it between here and San Pedro?"

"I think so. We should be able to get strong signals from the high powered broadcast stations pretty much all the way. Between KGO here locally, and KNX or KFI in the L.A. area we should have good DF coverage for the A and N homer signals."

"Well," Ford grinned and the crow's feet around his eyes seemed to crease a little more, "just pick one with some good music!" With that he turned and went forward to the cockpit.

Across the aisle in the right seat First Officer Thomas N. White, Sr. looked up from the operations manual lying open in his lap. "Ready for pre-flight checks when you are, Skipper."

White had not been originally scheduled for this flight. Ford's regularly scheduled First Officer, John Mack, had called in earlier to report that he would be unable to make the flight. Crew dispatch had to hurriedly locate another First Officer to take his place. When they discovered that Tom White was at Treasure Island attending a training class, they called him out of class, instructed him to go home, put on his uniform and report for duty as Ford's First Officer in time for the 3 P.M. scheduled departure. John Mack would be scheduled the next day and take the Honolulu shuttle flight where he would catch up with Ford for the flight south to New Zealand.

"Okay, Tom. Just let me get my manual out."

Ford reached for his thick black leather flight case, unsnapped the latch and withdrew the pre-flight checklist. Then he removed a flat, sealed envelope and carefully placed it in the inside breast pocket of his uniform jacket. As he did so, White glanced over and noticed that the envelope had large black cryptic letters stamped on it. "PLAN A – TOP SECRET – FOR CAPTAIN'S EYES ONLY". Ford had been handed the envelope by the flight dispatcher in the operations office only a few minutes earlier.

For the last couple of months Pan American's top management had been working with Army and Navy brass to formulate a contingency plan in the possible eventuality of the outbreak of war between the United States and Japan. Pan Am's fleet of large flying boats, providing as they would, essential aerial transport capacity in the Pacific, would present a tempting target for either capture or destruction by Japanese forces. Without knowing precisely where or when hostilities might begin, it was necessary to keep the plan flexible, up-to-date, and very top secret. Even so, it had become a source of common hangar flying talk among the flight crews that each flight leaving the mainland had, as a routine part of its pre-flight documentation, this flat, thin, legal-size envelope containing secret instructions as to what course of action to follow when – and the emphasis was on WHEN, not on if – the Japanese attacked.

As each captain arrived at the dispatch office on Treasure Island he was handed one of the envelopes for which he had to sign off on a special log. It was then his responsibility to ensure the security of that document for the duration of his flight assignment, returning it unopened to Dispatch if nothing had happened to require revealing its contents.

"Hmm," White joked, "looks like we're heading off into spy-in-the-sky country!"

"Just never mind, Tom!" Ford brought him up short. "That envelope is nobody's business...not even mine. I don't know what's in there and I don't even want to know unless we get word to look at it. Take my advice: just forget you ever saw it!"

White was momentarily taken aback by Ford's stern response. Bob Ford was usually pretty easy-going. Something in his Captain's tone told him that he had better not pursue the matter any further – not even in jest. "Okay," he replied meekly. Then, after a pause to regain his composure, "Ready for checklist when you are, Skipper."

"Just as soon as we have a head count," Ford replied. "Check that all stations are manned with the departure crew, confirm passenger loading complete and clear the dock area for cast off."

By now the rest of the crew had assumed their respective stations. Those First Officers who would man operating positions for departure settled into their locations and one by one checked in with the cockpit via the intercom.

"Rothe ready at engineering." First Engineering Officer Homans K. "Swede" Rothe called in from the engineer's station.

"Henricksen at navigation – course plotted and ready." James G. Henricksen, Third Officer, checked in.

"Hendrickson at radio. Radio ground checks completed."

Ford flipped his intercom to connect with the galley below the flight deck. "Barney, are you there?"

"Here, Skipper," the voice from the galley replied. Barney Sawicki would be Flight Steward for the trip, along with his assistant, Verne C. Edwards.

"How's the passenger loading coming?" Ford asked.

"All passengers are aboard. The gangway has been rolled back to the dock and the main entry hatch is being secured now."

"Fine, Barney."

Ford turned and looked toward the rear of the flight deck where the remaining crew members had gathered. "Steers, Parrish," he called, "man the bow compartment for cast off."

John D. Steers, Fourth Officer, and John B. Parrish, Second Engineering Officer, moved forward and down between the pilots' seats through the bow hatchway. There, they would await the signal to throw off the bow lines that secured the ship to the dock. Ground service personnel in a small dinghy positioned themselves in the water just behind the aft line attached to the rear of the fuselage. Another dinghy pulled up alongside the bow, ready to hand up the line they would use to tow the flying boat to the startup buoy.

Second Officer Roderick Norman Brown and Jack Poindexter were the only remaining crew members without an assigned duty for departure. They settled into the two seats at the rear of the flight deck.

Satisfied that all was ready for cast-off, Ford glanced over at White. "Okay, Tom, let's do it."

White peered through his windscreen toward the bow hatch and signaled Parrish and Steers to cast off the bow lines. When that was done the ground crew in the forward dinghy handed up the towing line and it was secured to the bow post. At the same time, the crew in the aft dinghy released the tail line. Now free of landside restraints, the Clipper was towed slowly forward to a buoy moored in the middle of the sheltered lagoon between Treasure Island and Yerba Buena Island. Once secured there, they were ready for engine start.

Following the litany of pre-start, engine, and flight control check list items, Ford punched the starter button for the Number One engine.

Suddenly the flight deck was filled with the high-pitched whine of the starter as it began to turn the engine. The big Hamilton Standard propeller started to revolve; slowly at first, then more rapidly as the engine picked up speed. After a few seconds the whine was replaced by the rough, coughing pulses of 14 cylinders coming to life. Grey-white puffs of smoke spewed from the exhaust stacks. The sound grew louder. The puffs of smoke dissipated. The pulses were replaced by a smoother, burr-like throb as the engine hit its stride. The exhaust stacks started their rhythmic thrumming.

Quickly, the same engine-start procedures were applied to the Number Four engine. Again, the same whine of the starter, the same rumbling to life of 1,600 more horsepower as Number Four added its voice to the swelling sound that now pervaded the cabin. As the engine came up to speed, White signaled Parrish to throw off the bow line. NC18606 was now a free agent, moving under its own power.

In quick succession, the port (left) inboard engine – Number Two – and the starboard (right) inboard engine – Number Three – added to the chorus of power.

Ford scanned the engine instruments on the cockpit panel. "Engineer, confirm oil pressure on all engines. Check idle rpm, mixtures all rich."

First Engineer Rothe's voice came through Ford's headset over the now constant rumble of the engines. "Oil pressures check okay, rpm at idle, mixtures rich. Ready for run-up."

"Ready for run-up and mag check," Ford repeated.

"Roger, Skipper," Rothe responded. "Run-up rpm and manifold pressure coming up on Number Two."

Ford motioned to White. "Mag checks, Number Two."

As White called out the settings, Ford watched out of his side window for any external indications of abnormal operation. Swede Rothe concentrated on the engine instruments on the big panel in front of him. "Rpm drops normal, manifold pressure normal, cylinder head temperatures normal and generator output looks good."

"Okay, check Number Three."

In a similar manner each of the other engines' ignitions, rpms, manifold pressures, and general readiness were checked.

White switched from intercom to radio. "PAN AM DISPATCH, THIS IS CLIPPER 18606. READY TO TAXI TO THE TAKEOFF CHANNEL."

(It should be noted here that Pan American pilots never used the Clipper's public relations name – i.e., *Pacific Clipper* – in official radio communications. The term *Clipper* plus the aircraft's registration or trip number was always the official way to identify the aircraft in radio communications).

"CLIPPER 18606, PAN AM DISPATCH. ROGER, TAXI TO THE EAST END OF THE BAY BRIDGE CHANNEL. WIND WEST 12, TEMPERATURE 56 DEGREES, ALTIMETER 29.82. THE CHANNEL TENDER REPORTS LIGHT CHOP. CHANNEL HAS BEEN SWEPT AND REPORTED CLEAR."

"ROGER, DISPATCH. STANDING BY FOR ATC CONFIRMATION," White replied. At the same time he gave a thumbs-up to Ford.

"ATC CLEARANCE REMAINS AS FILED IN THE DISPATCH OFFICE. DEPART AT YOUR DISCRETION AND CONTACT ATC WHEN AIRBORNE."

White clicked his microphone button twice in quick succession as a shorthand way of acknowledging the transmission by the dispatcher.

BOEING B-314 FLIGHT DECK

Captain's throttles and flight controls on the B-314

The space between the pilots' seats was used as the passageway from the flight deck to the bow compartment. Therefore, it was not possible to have a centrally located control pedestal. Each pilot had a small console located outboard of each seat containing a set of throttles. The Captain's throttles were at his left hand while the

First Officer's throttles were at his right hand. Accordingly, Bob Ford reached down with his left hand and grasped the four throttle lever handles. Slowly he eased them forward. "Increase rpm to taxi speed, Swede," he called over the intercom to the First Engineer.

Slowly at first, then with gathering speed, NC18606 moved toward the Berkeley shoreline at the far end of the Bay Bridge. Down below, the passengers heard the rhythmic slap-slap of the water against the bottom of the hull and watched the occasional dash of spray blow over the leading edges of the sea wings. As the big ship reached the far end of the takeoff channel, Ford swung it around in a wide arc.

"PAN AM DISPATCH, 06 READY FOR TAKEOFF."

"CLIPPER 06, ROGER, FINAL WIND CHECK, 240 DEGREES 11 KNOTS, CLEARED FOR TAKEOFF."

"Okay, Swede," Ford called over the intercom, "wing flaps set for takeoff, set cowl flaps for takeoff, follow me through on throttles for full takeoff power."

"Roger, Skipper. Cowl flaps set. Applying full power – NOW!"

The full-throated roar of the four engines filled the cabin as NC18606 moved forward into the takeoff run. The slap-slap of the water under the hull became a staccato drum beat. Spray whipped higher over the sea wings. After a few seconds the hull began to rise out of the water but was not quite free. Ford held the yoke steady as the airspeed indicator displayed the increasing speed: 40 knots... 50... 60... 70...

At 70 knots Ford brought the yoke back gently. The Clipper nosed up. Passengers seated in the aft compartments might have thought they were about to submerge as the tail came close to the water and the spray hurtling back from the sea wings splattered the windows. At 75 knots Ford eased up a little on the yoke then immediately brought it back. This rocking motion was necessary to raise the ship "on the step" – that area of the hull which would be the last to break free from the clinging suction effect of the water now hurtling along underneath the ship. As the airspeed went to 80 knots the sound of the water abruptly ceased. The thrumming beat against the hull was replaced by a sudden smoothness as the great ship broke free and began climbing.

"Flaps 10 degrees, throttle back to climb." Ford called to Rothe. The full-throated roar subsided slightly as the engineer backed off from the full power setting and the ship was trimmed for climb.

As soon as they reached 500 feet, Ford began a wide, sweeping turn to the right. At 1,000 feet he continued the turn until they were heading back toward the Berkeley side of the Bay. Finally, as they continued to climb, he set the ship on course toward San Pedro, some 350 miles to the south-southeast, and serving as the flying boat base for the Los Angeles metropolitan area.

B314 Takeoff (Pan American Airways photo).

In Warm Springs, Georgia, following an urgent telephone call from Secretary of

23

State, Cordell Hull, President Franklin D. Roosevelt cut short his vacation plans and boarded the Presidential train for a hurried return to Washington. (New York Times, Tuesday, December 2, 1941).

Somewhere between Hitukappu Bay in the Kurile Islands and Lat 40°N, Long 170°W a Japanese task force consisting of six carriers, two battleships, three cruisers and several destroyers and tankers, under the command of Vice Admiral Chuichi Nagumo, steamed steadily toward the rendezvous point from which they would head south towards Hawaii, maintaining strict radio silence.[1]

---

[1] Prange, Gordon W., <u>At Dawn We Slept – The Untold Story of Pearl Harbor</u>, McGraw-Hill Books, New York, 1981, p. 387

CHAPTER II
HONOLULU BOUND

The flight to San Pedro took about an hour longer than usual. Jack Poindexter asked Ford to fly on several different headings to check out the accuracy of the new radio homing equipment. By the time they had completed all tests and were squared away to approach and land at San Pedro Harbor, it was already late afternoon. They landed routinely, tied up at the harbor buoy and were taken ashore. A bus for the passengers and a crew limo were waiting for them on the pier.

"Thanks for the checkout on those new receivers." Ford remarked to Poindexter as they rode to the hotel where the crew would be put up for the night.

"Sure thing, Bob. Everything looks pretty well up to specs. You might want to keep a log for me while you're out along the line. Just some notes maybe, on when and where you used it and how well it worked; especially for approach patterns."

"Be glad to. You heading right back to San Francisco tonight?"

"Yeah. As soon as they drop you guys at the hotel. The limo driver said he'd give me a lift to Burbank to catch TWA to Oakland."

When they arrived at the hotel, while the crew was checking in, Poindexter went to a pay phone in the lobby. He placed a collect call to his wife in San Francisco.

"Hi, honey, it's me."

"Jack, where are you? You said to hold dinner, but it's getting pretty late. Is anything wrong?"

"No, hon, I'm still in L.A. The radio checkouts took longer than expected. I'm at the crew hotel now, but I'll be getting a ride to

Burbank. I should be able to get TWA out of there for Alameda. Ought to be home around eleven tonight."

"Eleven? So late!"

"I'm sorry, honey, but that's about the best I can do right now. Don't worry. I'll get a cab home from the airport. You won't have to come get me."

"Okay, I guess. What about supper?"

"I'll pick up something at the airport restaurant. Don't have to worry about holding that dinner for me."

"Okay, dear. Have a good flight."

"I will. Oh, and don't wait up for me. It'll probably be close to midnight by the time I get home. Love ya!"

"Love you too, Jack."

Each paused for a moment. Then Jack Poindexter hung up. As he turned away from the telephone booth he glanced toward the front desk. Oscar Hendrickson was standing there, beckoning to him.

"Yeah, Oscar, what's up?" Poindexter asked as he strolled toward the desk.

"Jack, we've got a problem here...," Hendrickson paused.

"Oh? What problem?"

"Harry Strickland was supposed to have joined us here as Second Radio Officer, but they say he was taken to the hospital early this afternoon with what looks like a bad case of appendicitis. Haven't been able to confirm it yet but, if it's true, he's going to be out of commission for a while. How do we handle it?"

Poindexter thought a moment. The loss of the Second Radio Officer would mean that Hendrickson would have to man the radio desk full-time. That would mean at least 15 to 18 hours on continuous duty on the next flight leg scheduled for tomorrow. If anything happened to him while en route there would be no backup radio operator. Pan Am's flight regulations were very specific and very strict: no flight could be cleared without double crew coverage for every position. There was only one answer: they had to find a replacement.

"Well, Jack," Hendrickson reasoned, "we can't go without two radio officers. As far as I know there's no other layover crew here in San Pedro. We could call San Francisco and have them try to find someone to send down. But that would be kind of 'iffy' considering how long it would take to get someone down here in time to leave with us tomorrow. I don't see anything for it, except that you'll have to come along."

"Oh, great!" Poindexter grimaced, "I just got through talking to my wife. Told her I'd be home around midnight tonight. Now she'll really be tee'd off!"

Hendrickson smiled ever so slightly at Poindexter. "Do you have any better idea?"

Poindexter admitted that they had very little choice in the matter. "Well, if I gotta, then I guess I gotta. Better get back on the phone again." And with that he turned back to the telephone booth.

NC18606 swung lazily at her mooring as the flight crew came aboard, followed by the passengers. The late afternoon sun shone brightly on the hull of the Boeing. Flickering patches of sunlight, reflecting off the water, dappled the underside of the high wing. This would be the longest over-water leg of the flight schedule: some 2,400 statute miles to the Pearl Harbor terminal at Honolulu. This was – and still is the longest over water commercial air route in the world with no alternate landing field. Since arriving the afternoon before, the Clipper had been subjected to an almost continuous round of activities which would make her ready for the trip. Fuel tanks had been topped with 100 octane aviation gas. Extra stores of food and water had been taken on board, and all four engines had been thoroughly inspected by Pan Am mechanics. It remained only for the crew to take charge, assume their respective duty stations and bring the big ship to life once again.

Because Poindexter was the Division's Chief Flight Radio Officer, he was designated as First Radio Officer while Oscar Hendrickson took over as Second Radio Officer. Poindexter took his place at the radio desk. This is going to be one hell of a long trip, he thought to himself, and I don't even have any extra clothes. There ought to be a better way...

When all the passengers had come aboard, Clipper 18606 took off on the second leg of its flight. Lifting off the harbor, Ford pointed the ship upward and headed west in accordance with the heading provided by the navigation officer. Once established on course, with all four engines droning steadily at their long-range cruise settings, there would now be time to relax a bit. Ford unfastened his seat belt and motioned to Tom White to take the left seat. Rod Brown now assumed White's former station in the right seat. "You've got the watch, Tom," Ford advised his First Officer. "Rotate with Brown and Henricksen the next three hours. If you need me, I'll be below."

Ford descended the spiral stairs to the main cabin and went forward to the galley. Barney Sawicki and Verne Edwards were busy preparing the evening meal.

"Something smells pretty good," Ford commented. "What's the menu for tonight?"

"Baked chicken, baked potato, peas and carrots, Skipper," Barney replied. "And Devil's food cake for dessert."

"Sounds great, Barney. Do you think you could spare an advance cup of coffee?"

"Sure, just a second." Sawicki turned to the coffee urn sitting on the sideboard, selected a mug from the cabinet and drew a cup of coffee which he handed to Ford.

"Thanks, Barn." Ford took the cup. Then, after a few sips, he peered down the length of the passageway toward the passenger compartments. "I guess it's time to do the PR chore," Ford mused, as he finished his coffee. "I'll be back in the main lounge. How long to dinner service?"

"We can start serving in about a half hour, Skipper."

Ford strolled back toward the main lounge. As he passed each section he stopped and introduced himself to the passengers.

First Officer Tom White, settled comfortably in the left cockpit seat, scanned the instruments in front of him. He tweaked the autopilot trim to compensate for a slight drift in the gyro compass. The compass heading, according to the small square of paper that Third Officer Jim Henricksen had taped to the brow of the instrument panel, was supposed to be 260 degrees. The gyro had drifted slightly during climb to altitude and was now showing 263. In a few seconds the gyro heading and the little square of paper were in agreement.

White relaxed a little and was contemplating the scene on the horizon. Sunset over the Pacific had a special quality, he thought. At their cruising altitude of 8,000 feet, they were now well on top of the broad deck of strato-cumulus that seemed to hover off the California coastline at this time of year. To the west a line of towering cumulus buildups loomed over the horizon, signaling the presence of an approaching cold front. Well, White thought, looks like the weather boys in Dispatch called this one pretty well. In the pre-flight briefing, Pan Am's meteorologist had forecast there might be a cold front

28

approaching the coast. The few reports from surface ships had indicated some shift in winds about 300 miles west of San Pedro. We'll have to watch those buildups pretty close, White thought. If we can't top 'em we may have to drop down beneath 'em.

Up above, a few scattered alto-cumulus clouds picked up the orange-lavender glow of the setting sun, now just below the horizon. Directly above the Boeing and toward the east, the warm glow faded to blue and then purple and then indigo, as sunset caught up with and passed the ship. The Boeing was holding a long-range cruise speed of 130 knots.

"Say, Tom, do we have a time to ETP[2] yet?" Second Officer Rod Brown's question broke through White's reverie.

White looked over at Brown, seated in the right seat. "Not yet, Rod. Why don't you check with Jim?"

Brown swung to his left and parted the night curtain that now hung between the cockpit and the main section of the flight deck. He stepped down and back toward the navigation table, being careful to re-secure the night curtain. The cockpit area had to be shielded from the lights on the main area of the flight deck so that the on-duty pilots could retain their night vision.

Third Officer Jim Henricksen was hunched over the map table, maneuvering a set of parallel rulers along the plotted track on the Mercator Projection.

"Do we have a time to ETP yet, Jim?"

"Just coming up... Wait a sec." Henricksen said, without looking up from his work. "Need to work in that last drift sight we took just before sunset and figure the wind drift from it. Still too much twilight for a good celestial, so we're trying radio fixes with the new A-N homer receivers.... Hey, Jack, you got those bearings yet?"

Jack Poindexter, at the radio desk, was concentrating on the dials of the two identical receivers in front of him. He slowly turned the DF loop control as he listened to the Morse Code signal, superimposed on the broadcast signal by the receiver, for the letter "A" to blend with the signal for the letter "N". Letter "A" was a dot and a dash; letter "N" was a dash and a dot. When the signals from the two sectors were equal they blended into one long, continuous tone. That would

---

[2] ETP: Equi-time Point is that point in a flight where, in the event of an engine failure, the flight time to destination is the same as the flight time back to the departure point.

be the "on course" relative bearing and he could then compute the magnetic bearing from the aircraft to the ground station. "Bearing zero-seven-three on KNX. Stand by for cross reading. I think I can get KGO pretty good now." Poindexter dialed in the frequency for the clear channel broadcast station in San Francisco. In a couple of seconds he heard music. The dial reading was confirmed a second later when the announcer came on with the call sign. Poindexter switched the function switch from voice to homer. Again he slowly turned the DF loop as the A-N homer circuit superimposed the Morse Code signals on the broadcast signal. In a few seconds he had his on-course reading. "KGO bearing zero-three-five. Okay, Jim?"

Henricksen took down the bearings and began plotting them on the chart. The intersection of the two on-course signals would give them a pretty good fix. Then, with the drift sight reading and the dead reckoning figures based on takeoff time and airspeed, he had the wind factor dialed onto the plotter. "Looks good, Jack, thanks." Within a minute or two he took out his pencil and made an "X" on the course line laid out on the chart. Next to it he jotted down the time: "13:12 GMT"[3]

Brown stared down at the notation. "That's it? 13:12?"

"Yep. Give or take a couple of minutes."

"Okay, thanks." Brown turned toward the cockpit, carefully parted the night curtain – just enough so that he could slip behind it – secured it again and returned to the right seat. "ETP at 13:12, Tom."

White glanced at the clock on the instrument panel. It showed 05:25. Another seven hours and forty minutes or so, he thought. That sounds about right unless that weather up ahead louses up the winds aloft. Better keep an eye on those buildups.

Jack Poindexter switched off the A-N homer function and changed to the air-ground channel. His next duty would be to contact KSF, the C.A.A. Overseas Communications Station at San Francisco. All overseas flights were required to report in at 15-minute intervals while over the ocean. If any overseas flight failed to meet that time limit, air traffic control would assume a cautionary communications alert status on the flight. If it missed two or more contact schedules, Search and Rescue would be alerted. At every 30-minute interval the

---

[3] GMT: Greenwich Mean Time. All overseas flights used Greenwich Mean Time (Now referred to as Universal Time) as the standard time reference for navigation and communications.

flight radio officer would transmit the Clipper's position, altitude, speed, and current weather conditions, as entered into the ship's log by the navigator.

"Coming up on the half-hour contact, Jim." Poindexter called to Henricksen. "You got that PX report ready?"

"Right up. Just have to insert the weather data."

Henricksen jotted a few last comments on the log sheet and handed it to Poindexter. Jack glanced briefly at the form to see that all was in proper order. Then he flipped on the transmitter switch.

It took Poindexter about two minutes to transmit the report, using the high-speed "bug" that most of Pan Am's radio operators carried on their flights. Anyone conversant with Morse Code could tell when a Pan Am operator was on the circuit; they were among the fastest Morse Code operators around. Pan Am's stringent training required a checkout at a minimum of 30 words per minute sending and receiving. The savvy of Pan Am's flight radio officers was unchallenged whenever Morse Code communications were used.

When he was finished with the radio contact, Poindexter had time to sit back and relax for a few minutes before the next quarter-hour contact was due. Ever since leaving San Pedro he had been puzzling over the sudden turn of events that had caught him unprepared for a long journey out along the line. Ford and his crew were scheduled for a one-day layover in Honolulu before picking up another B-314 and heading for Auckland, New Zealand. The round trip would take a little over two weeks. Poindexter would have to make do with only the clothes he was wearing. Well, he figured, maybe I'll have time to run down to Liberty House and pick up a spare shirt. Then he thought of his wife. What would she think of his sudden absence? Then he wondered if he had enough money with him. He took out his wallet and counted its contents. Hmm, just 36 dollars and eleven cents, he noted. I guess it's short rations from here on down unless I can get one of the ops boys to wangle me an advance. Talk about traveling light!

Down below, Barney Sawicki and Verne Edwards were serving dinner to the first group of passengers in the main lounge.

Bob Ford had greeted most of the passengers by now, exchanging introductions and pleasantries. But this 'PR chore', as he called it, was not his favorite in-flight activity. The company always encouraged the Captain of each flight to make an effort at getting acquainted with the passengers. They claimed that it helped reinforce the passengers' sense of safety and comfort to see a self-assured flight Captain, relaxed and pleasant, mingling with them. But Bob Ford preferred the company of his crew and the stimulation of the flight operations. Soon after dinner service began he excused himself and returned to the flight deck.

"How's the flight progress, Jim?" Ford asked as he came up the stairwell and stepped over to the navigator's table.

"Okay so far," Henricksen answered, "but we may have to change altitude soon. We've got what looks like the makings of a strong front up ahead and there may be others further west. Tom spotted some fairly large buildups on the horizon just before dark and it looked like they were just getting started. The tops could be too high for us to go over, so we may have to descend to go under 'em. Don't have a handle on cloud bases yet, but we might have to consider getting pretty low. Could be a bit rough down there too."

Ford stood silent for a moment, digesting what his Third Officer had just said. The Boeing was a big, strong ship, but frontal buildups were not to be fooled around with. If the storm front extended above the Boeing's rated service ceiling of 19,600 feet it would be beyond the aircraft's ability to stay above the clouds. Most likely they would have to descend below the cloud bases. That would mean stronger headwinds. This could be a longer flight than anticipated, he thought. "How about celestial fixes? Can we get some solid ones before we have to descend? Might not be able to get star sights if we'll be under an overcast for most of the flight."

"Yeah, I'm fixing to get those now. Figure another 20 to 30 minutes at this altitude. We can get a couple of celestials before we have to start down."

Henricksen reached for a large wooden case stowed under the chart table. He opened it and took out the octant. The octant was similar to a ship's sextant that mariners used to fix their position by star sightings. But it had been modified with its own internal bubble level and light source to provide a more visible and stable 'horizon' reference line for use aboard aircraft. Taking the octant in hand, Henricksen turned toward the cockpit and poked his head through the night curtain. "Hey, Tom, I'm going to run a couple of star sights. Hold her 'steady as she goes' for me for a few minutes, okay?"

Tom White glanced back at his crewmate. "Sure thing. Just holler when you're done." He then disengaged the auto-pilot and took manual control. The auto-pilot did a tolerable job of holding a

32

steady course, but it had a tendency to 'hunt' as the gyro-compass drifted slightly, and had to be fine-tuned every few minutes. By going on manual control, White would be able to hold the ship on a steadier keel while the navigator took his star sightings.

Henricksen turned and went to the rear of the flight deck. He opened the hatch to the cargo compartment and stepped through to the short ladder leading up to the navigator's dome. Steadying himself on the upper rungs, he grasped the octant with both hands and looked out into the now-black sky. The great expanse of wing extended left and right, tapering to slender tips. The transparent blue exhaust flames flickered out behind dull-red exhaust stacks. Above, the blackness was studded with uncountable stars across the entire hemisphere of sky. To the west, intermittent flashes of lightning illuminated and silhouetted the cumulus buildups. The tops of these frontal monsters were now approaching 25,000 feet – much too high for the B-314 to climb over. They would have to descend and pass beneath them. Better get these star sightings locked in now, Henricksen thought. Once we're under those buildups it's going to have to be dead reckoning for the rest of the night. He flipped on the octant's horizon light and began the sightings.

Navigator's dome in cargo compartment behind the flight deck (Pan American Airways photo).

Twenty minutes later Henricksen looked up from the chart table and called to Bob Ford. "Skipper, come take a look at this."

Ford rose from the seat at the rear of the flight deck where he had been checking engine logs with Swede Rothe. He came forward to the navigator's table. "What's up, Jim?"

"That sequence of star sights I took a while ago were all pretty solid, but if they're right, it looks like we have a stronger headwind than originally forecast. This line of position shows us with about a negative 15 component. I've had to revise ETP by a couple of hours. It's no problem as far as fuel reserve is concerned, but it will put us into Pearl a lot later than anticipated."

"About how much later?"

"Not much before noon or 1 p.m. Hawaii time."

"I guess we'll just have to settle for that. Might as well get your duty relief shifts set up for a long night and morning. I'll relieve Tom White now and you and he might as well go below. Get some dinner and then sack in for a while. We'll make it three on, three off for the rest of the trip."

Ford went forward to the cockpit. He relieved White and Fourth Officer John Steers took Rod Brown's place in the right seat. Oscar Hendrickson took over the radio watch from Jack Poindexter. John Parrish relieved Swede Rothe at the engineer's station. With the watch change complete, the off-duty crew went below to eat and rest. The on-duty crew settled into their routines as the Boeing droned on, moving steadily toward the first of a series of cold fronts that lay across its flight path.

By this time, British, Dutch, and American naval forces were on alert throughout the Pacific. Australia was designated as a "war station". Small boats in Hawaii were put under license and Hong Kong's defenses were in place. A British fleet, headed by the battleship "Prince of Wales", arrived at Singapore. (New York Times, Tuesday, December 2, 1941)

CHAPTER III
A LONG NIGHT TO HONOLULU

At first the bumps had been slight and intermittent. But as the Boeing crossed the advancing wind-shear line, the turbulence increased. Ford ordered the engineer to throttle the engines back in preparation for penetrating the storm front. Airspeed now showed only 120 knots. If Henricksen's figure of a 15 knot negative component was accurate, that meant that their forward ground speed was down to about 105 knots, or a mere 115 miles per hour.

"Trim for descent, 500 feet per minute, John," Ford called to John Parrish. "Might as well get below that stuff now while we still have room to spare."

Gradually the big ship descended. At 3,000 feet they were still above the bases of the cumulus looming before them. "Keep it coming down," Ford ordered, "but put a stopper in it at 1,000 feet."

At 1,000 feet above the sea the Boeing leveled off. They had barely 500 feet of clearance to the cloud bases above. The turbulence, by now, was almost continuous: light, sometimes moderate bumps, accompanied by occasional staccato bursts of rain, loud enough to punctuate the drone of the engines.

Down below, most of the passengers had long since bedded down for the night. Some lay anxiously wakeful in their bunks, bracing for each sudden bump or lurch as the turbulent ride continued. Others, more experienced in such situations, slept comfortably, if not altogether soundly. The curtains closing off the bunks swayed with every small motion of the aircraft. The long passageway was dimly illuminated by a series of night lights. The entire aspect of the lower main deck was that of an abandoned ship. Not one soul was in sight throughout the length of the compartments. Assistant Flight Steward

Verne Edwards sat on a small seat in the galley section, nursing a cup of coffee. He was reading a magazine but kept an alert ear for the sound of the call buzzer that would mean that one of his charges needed assistance. Barney Sawicki was taking his turn in the bunk and another two hours would pass before they would trade places.

21 Degrees, 30 minutes North, 157 Degrees West. Noon Hawaii time. NC18606 had now been airborne for somewhat more than 21 hours. The cold fronts that had plagued her progress were now well to the east. Dawn, five hours earlier, had revealed a bright blue sky punctuated by brilliant white patches of small cumulus, typical of the trade wind pattern that signaled the approach to the Hawaiian Islands. With the passage into better weather, Ford had climbed back to a more comfortable cruising altitude of 6,000 feet. Rod Brown, taking his turn as navigator, was shooting a sun line from his perch in the navigator's dome.

Oscar Hendrickson, at the radio desk, was transmitting the latest position report to the C.A.A. station in Honolulu. When that task was done he flipped off the transmitter switch and stretched. It had been a long night and morning. He'd be glad to get to the Moana Hotel and relax on the beach for a while.

Soon they would be within range of the terminal voice control channel. Then the pilots would take over communications directly with ATC and the Pan American flight watch operator at Pearl City. Hendrickson switched one of the receivers to the commercial broadcast band and tuned in KGMB – the Honolulu clear channel station. The signal came in loud and clear just as the announcer was in the middle of a news broadcast.

> *"...no progress in bridging the gulf between the two countries with respect to their respective positions in the Far East. Furthermore, Secretary of State, Cordell Hull, indicated that Japan had not as yet responded to President Roosevelt's inquiry as to Tokyo's intentions in Indo-China. It has been Japan's contention that the transfer of Imperial forces to Indo-China was only for the purpose of maintaining law and order. According to Saigon sources,*

Japan had pledged not to send any additional troops, nor to use its present position there as a jumping-off point for attacks on Thailand or the Burma Road..."

What bullshit! Hendrickson thought. Just some more liar's poker talk. Can't believe anything you hear from any of those jokers. Wouldn't surprise me if the whole damn mess blew up in their faces.

"Hey, Oscar, can you set up the voice channel now?" It was Tom White, standing behind Ford's cockpit seat. "I think we should be within range now. I can just spot Koko Head coming up about five degrees off the port bow."

"Sure thing, Tom." Hendrickson switched one of the receivers to the terminal control channel and then did the same with one of the transmitters. He listened for a moment to check that the frequency was clear and then pressed his microphone button.

"PEARL CITY FLIGHT WATCH, PEARL CITY FLIGHT WATCH, THIS IS CLIPPER 18606. DO YOU READ? OVER."

"CLIPPER 18606, PEARL CITY, ROGER,LOUD AND CLEAR. GOOD MORNING TO YOU. OR SHOULD I SAY GOOD AFTERNOON... YOU BOYS ARE RUNNING A LITTLE LATE TODAY, AREN'T YOU?"

"ROGER ON THAT, PEARL. JUST SOME LITTLE OLD FRONTS ALONG THE WAY AS USUAL. NOTHING BIG BUT JUST ENOUGH TO SLOW US DOWN SOME. STAND BY - SWITCHING TO COCKPIT CONTROL. THE NEXT VOICE YOU HEAR WILL BE THAT OF OUR ILLUSTRIOUS FIRST OFFICER, TOM WHITE."

Hendrickson gestured to White. "Loud and clear on 2870 kilocycles. You can take it on the cockpit console now."

White nodded an "Okay" to Hendrickson, then turned toward the cockpit where Bob Ford was once again in the left seat. John Steers, who had been in the right seat for the past three hours, stepped out onto the flight deck and White took his place.

"Voice contact with Pearl, Skipper." White remarked as he secured his seat belt.

"Okay, get us cleared for approach. Do we have a landing direction yet?"

"The last weather report showed the wind as 60 degrees at about 26 knots. Pretty breezy."

"Check with Pearl for a sweep of the west-to-east landing area in East Loch, just north of Ford Island. That ought to be about right if the wind holds."

As soon as ATC cleared them for approach and landing, Ford ordered Swede Rothe to throttle back the engines. The Boeing began a gradual descent. At 2,000 feet they leveled off again and held that altitude as they came around the eastern tip of Oahu. Soon the familiar outline of Diamond Head came into view. As they passed Waikiki, White glanced down at the beach. The gleaming white Moana Hotel and the bright pink Royal Hawaiian Hotel were the only large buildings on the beachfront. The beach appeared to be almost deserted. Looks like a nice day for a swim, White mused to himself.

"Take her down to 1,000 feet for initial approach. Cowl flaps open, wing flaps 10 degrees, and let's get a final wind check and confirmation on channel sweep from the tender." Bob Ford's voice cut through White's thoughts.

White repeated the instructions and proceeded to make the necessary control adjustments. Then he picked up his microphone.

"PEARL, THIS IS CIPPER 06 – REQUEST FINAL WIND CHECK AND WE'D LIKE TO PLAN FOR LANDING WEST TO EAST IN EAST LOCH ON THE NORTH SIDE OF FORD ISLAND. REQUEST CHANNEL SWEEP AND CONFIRMATION FROM THE TENDER. OVER."

"CLIPPER 06 – ROGER. WIND NOW 050 DEGREES 15 GUSTING TO 25. GENERALLY LIGHT CHOP ON ALL CHANNELS. STAND BY – WE'LL GET THE TENDER OUT THERE MOMENTARILY."

It took a few minutes for the tender boat to make a sweep of the channel. Once it had been determined that the channel was clear of any floating debris and there was no surface traffic in the way, the flight watch operator radioed confirmation to the Clipper. By this time the Boeing was turning on its final approach leg over Ewa Beach.

"Full flaps, trim tabs set for approach. Swede, I'll take the throttles now for final," Ford called to the engineer.

Slowly the ship descended on the final approach leg. Passing over Waipio Peninsula they were down to 500 feet. As they came abeam of Ford Island, White glanced over to Battleship Row. The warships lined up there looked as though they were ready for a nautical parade. Standing out brightly against the dark blue waters of the harbor, they presented a formidable sight.

As they passed over Middle Loch, Ford gently eased back on the yoke until the Boeing's bow was about five degrees above the horizon. He eased the throttles back further. As the airspeed dropped to 80 knots, he trimmed to hold that speed. The ship descended more slowly now – 200 feet per minute... 100 feet per minute... 50 feet per minute.. feeling ever so gently for that moment of contact with the water.

Suddenly the smooth descent was interrupted by a light jolt, followed by the rapid slap-slap of water under the hull. Ford pulled the four throttles back to idle and held the yoke all the way back. The Boeing's tail dropped low to the surface as twin rooster-tails of spray catapulted rearward from the sea wings. The drag of the water quickly dissipated most of the forward landing speed. Ford let up on the yoke. The bow came down and the Boeing settled into its normal shallow draft attitude on the water.

John Steers and John Parrish once again came forward and climbed down through the bow hatch where they would receive the mooring lines from the tender. It took just a few minutes to turn around and taxi back to the dock area where the tender secured the bow lines to a mooring buoy.

"All controls to idle cutoff. All mag switches off, fuel pumps off, close fuel valves, main switch off, secure control gust locks." Ford called out the final housekeeping chores. As the big propellers wound down, the constant drone of the engines was replaced by silence and the occasional slap of water against the hull. They could hear the handling crew, outside, calling instructions to each other as they warped the now dormant craft alongside the dock and secured the gangway to the port sea wing. While the passengers were disembarking, the on duty crew members made final entries in their respective operating logs. With that duty finished, they left the aircraft and walked the short distance to the operations office where they finished up the necessary paperwork required by company procedures. Then they boarded the waiting crew limousine for the ride to Waikiki.

As soon as he had checked into his room at the Moana, Jack Poindexter sought out the desk clerk in the lobby. "I'd like to send a telegram to the Mainland. Can you handle it here?"

"Yes sir, we have a direct line to Western Union. Where do you want it to go?" the clerk replied as he handed Poindexter a pad of message forms.

"To my wife in San Francisco. Just a short line."

Poindexter penciled in the short message on the pad: 'ARRIVED HNL 1PM STOP ALL WELL STOP DEP FOR CANTON ISLAND 12/4 STOP MORE LATER STOP LOVE JACK'

He filled in name, address, and phone number information and handed the pad back to the clerk. The clerk silently counted the words and made a short entry in the service box. "That'll be two dollars and fifty cents, Mr. Poindexter."

Poindexter pulled out his wallet and handed over one of the larger bills. When the clerk handed him his change he looked at the now depleted wallet. Hmm, he thought, can't send too many of those at this rate. Better see if I can pick up at least one extra shirt before we leave for Canton.

With the message taken care of, Poindexter turned and walked down the main entrance steps to Kalakaua Avenue. He knew that the Honolulu bus ran right past the hotel and that it could take him to Liberty House in just a few minutes. Shouldn't cost too much for just one shirt, he thought, better do it now.

By this time several of the crew, including Tom White, Oscar Hendrickson, John Steers, Jim Henricksen, and Rod Brown, had changed into swim trunks, grabbed towels from their rooms, and were soaking up the sunshine on the beach. Members of other layover crews joined them and soon they had a vigorous volleyball game going.

Among those members was John Mack, who had missed leaving with Ford on the original departure from San Francisco. He had taken the "Honolulu Shuttle" flight the next day and was already in Honolulu when Ford and his crew arrived. It was arranged that Mack would take Tom White's place with Ford for the journey south to New Zealand, scheduled for the next day, and White would return with the shuttle crew to San Francisco.

Meanwhile, Bob Ford had also changed into beach wear, not to play volleyball but to go surfing. A few months earlier he had talked himself into buying a surfboard from the hotel manager. Now, during each layover in Honolulu, he was determined to master that Hawaiian sport. He had the desk clerk open the flight crew luggage storage room where the surfboard was stored. In a few minutes he was lying prone on the big plywood board and paddling out to the surf line where several other surfers sat, waiting to catch that one 'just right' swell that would give them a speedy and exhilarating ride to the beach.

Those crew members who had not opted for either volleyball or surfing, or just lying in the sun, soon congregated in the lobby near the bar. In short order the inevitable poker game started. It was mostly nickel, dime, quarter stuff, but it was surprising how fast some of the pots built up. With help from members of other layover crews, the limit of seven players was reached quickly. Later, as the game continued into the evening, some players dropped out and their seats were promptly taken by other crew members who had strolled by to observe the action.

"Okay, boys, it's five-card draw, jokers wild, jacks or better to open. Ante up!" Swede Rothe called as he took his turn at the dealer's choice game, now well under way at the big circular table on the Diamond Head portico overlooking the Banyan Court. With an unlit cigar clamped firmly in his teeth and his hands flying as he dealt the cards around the table, he looked like a river boat gambler plying his trade.

"I'll open for a quarter." Verne Edwards called out the first challenge for the hand.

"Call." John Parrish tossed his quarter into the pot.

Barney Sawicki slowly fanned the five cards inside his cupped palm "Hell, these mothers ain't worth a damn!" he said, disgustedly. "I'll sit this one out!" He slapped his cards face-down on the table and sat back to watch the action.

Seven hundred miles northwest of Oahu, Admiral Nagumo's task force proceeded at reduced speed through a winter storm that stirred the North Pacific. While the storm had forced them to slow to a more cautious pace, the cloud cover was a welcome sight: it would insure protection against early detection by any American aerial patrols that might stray into the area. And the strict radio silence imposed upon the fleet made detection by that means impossible.

NC18602 docked at Pan Am's Pearl City base in Pearl Harbor

CHAPTER IV
TO CANTON AND FIJI

Pearl City Base, December 4, 1941

Bob Ford stood at the briefing counter in the operations office and studied the meteorological chart just handed to him by the dispatcher. The serpentine lines of the pressure patterns and frontal weather locations drawn on the chart told him a story that he had seen before on this part of the South Pacific run.

"What do you make of this, John?" Ford asked as he slid the synoptic chart in front of First Officer John Mack, who was standing next to him at the counter. Not that he needed Mack's advice on how to interpret the map; he was simply interested to see if his First Officer's interpretation of the weather information coincided sufficiently with his own so that they would be of one mind when it came to the critical flight planning decisions necessary for a safe flight.

Mack stared at the chart for a long moment. "Well, Skipper, it looks like more of the same stuff we've usually run into on this run before. That pattern of upper-level westerlies extending along the Equator has a pretty steep gradient. The prevailing trades and south-easterlies are just about as strong. Looks to me like the Intertropical Front is going to be up and running like Gangbusters all along that line in a few hours. We just might be in for a bit of a wet, rough ride."

"Nothing we can't handle though, right?"

"Yeah, right... piece o' cake! Just thank the Lord for little favors... No icing to worry about!" Mack grinned at his Captain.

"Okay then. Let's go earn a living!"

Another Boeing – NC18602, the *Pacific Clipper* – had arrived at Pearl City the previous day on the direct San Francisco Honolulu Shuttle flight. This was the same flying boat that John Mack had been assigned to after having missed the initial departure with Ford. Now he was joining Ford and the rest of his crew on NC18602 for the flight south.

In anticipation of an early departure, a full load of gas, mail bags, and other cargo had been loaded aboard during the night. The handful of passengers continuing south had boarded about a half hour ago. Barney Sawicki and Verne Edwards had also gone on board at that time to see to their seating arrangements. Now, as the weather briefing concluded, Ford, Mack and the rest of the crew left the dispatch office, walked the short distance to the dock and went aboard.

Everyone settled quickly into the routines of their respective duties. Pre-flight checks were completed and in a few minutes NC18602 had come alive with the familiar rumble and vibration of the four Wright engines. At precisely 8 A.M. Ford gave the command. All lines were cast off, Ford eased the throttles forward and the big Boeing moved out to the takeoff channel.

"Local surface winds haven't come up yet," Ford observed. "I think we'd better plan on a takeoff to the south. Without a good headwind component for takeoff, at this gross weight our rate of climb would be pretty marginal for clearing those sugar cane fields to the north and east. Let's take it straight out the harbor entrance. That way we can hold a lower altitude until the airspeed builds up."

With that takeoff criteria as a guide, Mack made contact with Pan American flight watch and requested the appropriate clearance. By the time final mag checks had been completed, the clearance had been relayed from ATC. Once again Ford called to Swede Rothe for follow-through on the throttles. As the engines revved up to full takeoff power, the B-314 surged forward, spray flying. Once airborne, Ford continued due south, holding a couple of hundred feet of altitude until the airspeed built up sufficiently to allow for a standard rate of climb to their initial cruising altitude of 8,000 feet above sea-level. About an hour after takeoff, Barney Sawicki came up to the flight deck and went forward to the cockpit.

"Hi, Barn," Ford greeted him. "How's everything going downstairs?"

44

"All normal and routine, Skipper. Just thought you'd like to know we have some kind of VIP on board this trip."

"Oh, yeah? How 'Very Important'?"

"Sir Harry Luke, the British Governor-General of Fiji. According to this morning's edition of the *Honolulu Advertiser*, he's been attending some top-level meetings with the Navy brass. My guess is it has something to do with all this stuff going on with the Japs. He says this is his first ride in a Clipper. He wanted me to ask you if it would be okay for him to come up and see the flight deck."

"I guess we have to be diplomatic with the diplomats..." Ford replied. "Sure, show him on up. We'll give him the deluxe dollar tour."

"Okay, he's on his way." Barney turned and went down the stairs.

Within a couple of minutes another figure emerged from the stairwell: Sir Harry Luke, K.C.M.G., D. Litt, Governor-General of Fiji and Commissioner for the Western Pacific.

Ford stepped down from his seat. "Johnny, take the left seat for a while. I'll show our guest around." Then he turned toward the visitor and extended his hand. "Your Excellency, good morning. My steward informs me this is your first flight on a Clipper."

"Yes, that is so," Sir Harry replied, "and I can tell you I find it utterly fascinating! Really, you chaps have certainly got a wonderful machine here."

"We like to think of it as the latest advance in aircraft design. I understand that your British Overseas Airways has contracted to purchase three of these models for their trans-Atlantic run."

"Oh!" Sir Harry's eyebrows arched in surprise. "By Jove, I hadn't heard that. But then, news from home always seems to take a long time to reach us here in the colonies." And he laughed.

"Let me show you around a bit. Shall we start with the cockpit area and work back?"

"You're the Captain. Lead on, Sir."

Bob Ford invited his guest to sit in the co-pilot's seat while he described the functions of the various instruments and controls. When that area had been thoroughly explained, they stepped back to examine the other flight stations. When Ford showed him the hatchways leading into the wings, Sir Harry was duly impressed.

"I say, that is extremely clever. To be able to get to the engines like that in flight. Do you find it necessary to venture into that area often?"

"No, not very much," Ford explained. "It's used mainly to check the security of the hydraulic lines, fuel lines, and control cables. Any work on an engine would require that it be shut down and we don't do that very often en route. I suppose, in an emergency, you could do repair work in the accessory section just behind the firewall, but that would be about the extent of it. Actually, the people who get the most use out of it are the mechanics back at Treasure Island. It makes the hard-to-get-to places at the rear of the engine more accessible during routine maintenance inspections."

Sir Harry nodded, "Hmm, yes, I see... Still, a very clever idea, what?"

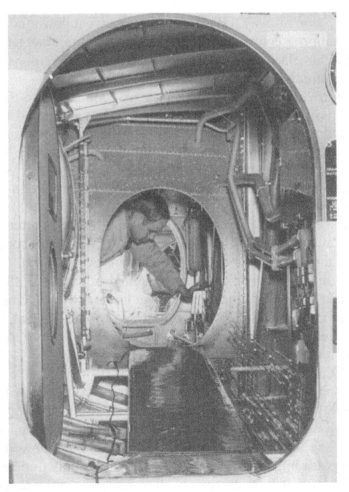

Catwalks inside wing leading edge provided access to engines in flight (Pan American Airways photo).

Finally, with the tour of the flight deck completed, the two men had little else to do except engage in polite small talk. This always made Ford uncomfortable. Years of habit and professional indoctrination inclined him to keep the progress of his flight commands uppermost in his mind. Social interaction with the passengers was always secondary. His sense of propriety, however, helped him to understand that this was no ordinary passenger, so he made a special effort to be cordial. He remembered what Barney Sawicki had said when he informed him of the Governor-General's presence on board.

"I understand that you've been conferring with our Naval Command at Pearl Harbor," Ford probed. "How do you see the present situation regarding Japan? It seems that all we hear nowadays are charges and counter-charges."

Sir Harry frowned slightly at this unexpected query. As a diplomat he was in that delicate position where, if he spoke too openly, he could be guilty of a breach of security, and yet, if he simply refused to comment at all, he could be thought to be hiding something. He paused several seconds before answering.

"Well, sir," he couched his words with care, "it is, of course, a very delicate situation. We have just finished a conference with CINCPAC[4] Headquarters which had been arranged between our Naval Commander at Fiji and your Pearl Harbor counterparts some months ago. It's just one of those uncanny coincidences that it comes at a time like this. Truthfully, I'd have to say that we are not really sure where all this running to and fro is going to end up. I would hope that your diplomats and the Japanese envoys would have the good sense to arrive at a mutually acceptable solution. We are, of course, concerned with the protection of our mutual interests in the Pacific. And, to a certain extent, I can tell you that our conference was for the purpose of examining those interests and arriving at some reasonable plan for protecting them in the event of any untoward hostilities. Beyond that, Captain Ford, I must beg your indulgence, as I am really not at liberty to discuss the issue any further."

"Of course, Your Excellency, I understand," Ford acquiesced. "I wouldn't expect you to breach any security issues."

Well, Ford thought, that pretty much closes that area of conversation. Now what the devil do we talk about?

---

[4] CINCPAC – "Commander-in-Chief Pacific"

The answer to that was literally Heaven-sent. Without any warning, the big craft dropped suddenly as it ran into a strong downdraft. And just as suddenly it felt as though they were in a high-speed elevator, heading upwards at rocket-like speed.

"Clear air turbulence, Skipper!" Johnny Mack called from the cockpit. "Better batten down the hatches. It looks like we're coming up on the first series of fronts. Got a lot of buildups out ahead of us."

Ford almost made an audible sigh of relief. This was his chance to cut loose from his guest.

"Sir Harry, I expect we may be in for a bit of rough weather for a while. I think it would be best if you returned below and belted yourself in. It's really been a pleasure to show you around. Perhaps, later, when we get clear of these fronts, we can chat again."

"Of course, Captain Ford, I understand. I wouldn't want to interfere with your duties. Thank you again for the tour. It was most delightful and informative." With that the two shook hands and Sir Harry descended the stairwell, carefully holding onto the handrail to brace himself against the suddenly turbulent ride.

For the next few hours they were in and out of a series of weather fronts that, at times, forced Ford to fly as low as 500 feet above the water through torrential rain showers. The flight deck and passenger cabin areas became hot and muggy as the Clipper threaded its way between the heavier build-ups. Finally, just as the sun had set and the short-lived tropical twilight was waning, the low-lying outline of Canton Island appeared on the horizon. In semi-darkness they landed in the lagoon, tied up at the buoy, went ashore, and checked in at the Pan American Hotel.

Sir Harry opted to spend the night as a guest of his British counterpart on the island – Canton being ruled over at the time by both the British and American governments in a sort of 'condominium' arrangement; the result of compromise negotiations between the United States and Great Britain. British and American sailors had both discovered Canton and the other small atolls of the Phoenix Group during the first half of the 19th century. Britain had annexed them in 1889. In 1938, when Canton became a strategic refueling point for the trans-Pacific Clipper flights, the United States had claimed Canton and Enderbury Islands as U.S. possessions. Subsequent negotiations with Great Britain by Pan Am's astute president, Juan Trippe, had resulted in this marriage of convenience, entered into in 1939 and scheduled to last for fifty years.

The following day, December 5th, dawned bright and hot. Cumulus buildups were already visible in every direction around the horizon. The combination of dazzling white clouds and glaring coral surface made the use of sunglasses almost mandatory. At only two degrees south of the Equator, the tropical sun was a blinding, palpable presence, even immediately after sunrise.

Once again, passengers and crew boarded NC18602. This next leg would be one of the shorter hops. From Canton to Suva, Fiji was little more than 1,100 miles. If they departed early enough to avoid the most active period of the Intertropical frontal zone they would be able to maintain an altitude that afforded more favorable winds aloft. As the big craft taxied slowly away from the buoy toward the far end of the seaplane channel, Second Officer Rod Brown, taking his turn at the navigator's station, carefully plotted the course on the Mercator chart. Before they had reached the takeoff position he noted the initial flight heading on a small square of paper and attached it to the brow of the instrument panel with a piece of cellophane tape.

"Initial heading after takeoff should be 210 degrees, Skipper," Brown informed Ford.

"Okay, Rod. And what does our flight time look like?"

"Provided we can hold our flight-planned altitude, 8 hours and 35 minutes ought to be just about on the money."

"Okay, let's go!" Ford replied as he motioned to Swede Rothe at the engineer's station. As always, the flight engineer and the captain began their coordinated moves, each following through on his own set of engine throttles to begin the takeoff run.

The tiny atoll was quickly lost to view in the tropical haze and glare of the early morning sun. NC18602 climbed away and headed south-southwest. When they reached 8,000 feet, Ford leveled off. As soon as the aircraft was trimmed and the autopilot engaged, he turned the watch over to Johnny Mack and went below to cadge his habitual cup of coffee from the galley.

"Morning, Skipper," Verne Edwards greeted him as he came into the galley area. "The usual?"

"Yeah, Verne, Make it a hot one, black, no sugar."

Edwards filled the cup and handed it to Ford.

"How is our VIP passenger doing this morning?" Ford asked.

"Sir Harry? Oh, he's doing fine. By the way, he asked me if it would be okay with you if he visited the flight deck again when we get within sight of Fiji. Says he's never really seen his domain from the air before."

"I guess we can arrange that. I'll send word down when we have the island in sight."

Ford finished his coffee and returned to the flight deck. For the next few hours the flight was smooth and routine. The early morning departure from Canton had helped to avoid the daily buildup of frontal activity characteristic of the Equatorial area. Shortly after passing their ETP position they crossed the International Dateline and promptly lost one full day on the calendar. The had left Canton on December 5th. They would arrive at Suva on December 6th, even though the flight time would be only eight and a half hours.

After several rotations of watch duty, Bob Ford was once again in the left seat with Johnny Mack on his right. Approach and landing charts were retrieved from flight cases. The two pilots reviewed the arrival and landing procedures that would bring them into Suva.

"We'll need clearance down to about 2,500 feet from about twenty miles out," Ford commented. "Most likely there will be that cloud cap over the mountains and we'll have to get below it for a visual approach."

"Right," Johnny Mack acknowledged. "I'll get on 2870 to Dispatch as soon as we have voice range."

When the first grey outline of Viti Levu, one of Fiji's two larger islands, appeared on the horizon, Ford sent word down to the galley to have Sir Harry come to the flight deck. In a few minutes, the Governor-General presented himself to Ford.

"Captain, thank you so much for this opportunity."

"That's quite all right, Your Excellency," Ford assured him. "You're most welcome."

Soon they were descending below the cloud bases and coming up on the northeast shore of the island.

"Sir Harry, if you look there," Ford said as he pointed diagonally out of the starboard section of the cockpit windscreen, "you should be able to make out Mount Tomaniivi. The top is in the clouds right now, but the lower slopes are quite visible."

Sir Harry peered in the indicated direction. "Ah, yes! By Jove that is a grand sight!"

Very shortly they were paralleling the coastline. Sir Harry could see the mangrove trees along the coast and, further inland, the sugar cane fields. Then the city of Suva came in view as Ford guided the Boeing around the entrance to the harbor for the final approach and landing. There were a number of other, smaller flying boats at anchor in the bay. Johnny Mack contacted Pan American flight watch and obtained landing clearance. They touched down on the water of Suva harbor within two minutes of Rod Brown's original estimated flight time.

They had arrived early enough so that, by the time they were taken ashore in the Pan Am launch, driven to the hotel, and checked in, there was still time to watch a cricket match going on in the park across from the hotel. Fourth Officer John Steers and Third Officer Jim Henricksen changed quickly to street clothes and headed out to watch the action.

"Let's pick up a couple of beers at the bar," Henricksen suggested, "and then watch the game."

The two passed through the hotel bar, picked up a bottle of beer each and strolled across to the park. Very soon, Henricksen was attempting, without much success, to explain the play of the game. Steers finally caught on to the idea that the bowlers were trying to put the batsmen "out" by hitting the wickets and knocking the bails off, while the batsmen were trying to score runs by batting the ball away. But the scoring rules seemed like so much gibberish. After about an hour of watching they both got up to return to the hotel. But as they rose from the bench, John Steers made a startling discovery: apparently, the section of the bench that he had sat down on had only recently been painted, and some of the paint had come off on his fresh, white suit. After some appropriate cussing and swearing, Steers finally resigned himself to turning the suit in to the hotel valet service for cleaning. But as circumstances would have it, they were scheduled to leave the next morning before the suit could be returned from the cleaners. Well, Steers thought, I'll just tell them to hold it until we get back on the return trip, and pick it up then. Little did he know that there would not be a return trip, and the fate of his new white suit would be forever unknown.

After supper, some of the crew members played a couple of rounds of poker before turning in for the night. Sleeping proved to be a little difficult. The hotel floor plan was very peculiar. All the rooms were 'inside' rooms with no windows. Ventilation was very poor and the heat and humidity made sleep fitful and elusive.

Two hundred miles north of the Hawaiian Islands, the Imperial Japanese attack force resumed a more direct course to a position due north of the island of Oahu. Still maintaining radio silence, Vice Admiral Nogumo's flagship sent flag and blinker signals to all vessels to make final preparations for launching the attack. They would reach their launch point within 36 hours.

CHAPTER V
NOUMEA, AUCKLAND, AND INFAMY

December 6, 1941 (December 7th in Suva)

The departure from Suva was a leisurely affair. This leg to Noumea, New Caledonia would take just a little over six hours. Following their usual routine, the crew met in the hotel dining room for breakfast. About an hour later they boarded the Pan American bus for the short ride to the harbor. NC18602 swung to and fro quietly, tethered to a buoy just off the main pier. The morning air was warm and humid. A few clouds were beginning to form over the mountain peaks, but away to the south and west the sky was clear.

"Good thing this will be a short leg," John Steers remarked as he stifled a yawn. "I sure didn't get much sleep last night. That's the dumbest room arrangement I've ever seen! Don't those Limeys believe in fresh air?"

"Maybe they're more concerned about keeping the mosquitoes out." Jim Henricksen conjectured. "Did you notice any in your room?"

"Well, no..."

"Besides, our next digs will have plenty of fresh air. Then you can sleep the whole stopover away."

"Oh, yeah? What would that be?"

"Oh, you'll see," Henricksen teased him. "Just wait 'til we get to Noumea."

As this was Steer's first flight assignment to the South Pacific run he could not imagine what Henricksen was alluding to. But he did not have much time to ponder the matter. Shortly after completing the pre-flight briefing at the Pan American dispatch office, the crew boarded the launch and rode out to the flying boat.

The ingrained routine of pre-flight checks, startup, cast-off procedures, and preparation for takeoff: all these required their complete attention. Any sense of fatigue induced by a poor night's sleep was overridden by the immediate demands of the flight operation. Once airborne and at altitude, the rotation of crew duties would give each crew member a brief time to relax in the forward crew compartment on the main deck. But this flight leg was so short that only two rotations of crew duties were required before they were landing in the harbor at Noumea.

John Steers once again wielded his boat hook from the bow hatch, captured the line from the mooring buoy and secured it over the snubbing post. As soon as the ground personnel had secured the Boeing to the dock the crew deplaned and Steers could see what Henricksen had meant. Pan American was still in the process of building complete passenger and crew accommodations at Noumea. As a temporary arrangement, they were leasing a large yacht – the Southern Seas – formerly owned by the Curtis Publishing Company. Tied up to the dock at Noumea, it was being used for overnight accommodations for the flight crews. This rather luxurious facility contributed to a certain 'party time' atmosphere as NC18602's crew checked in. They promptly doffed their uniforms in favor of swim wear for an afternoon and evening of sun-bathing on the deck, drinking beer, and swapping stories with the British and Australian members of the yacht crew.

> *By now, Japan was declaring that the United States note reaffirming the U.S. stand in the Pacific, to be 'utterly impossible'. The Japanese envoys to Washington were preparing to present President Roosevelt with an answer to that note. Roosevelt was conferring with Congressional leaders regarding the Far East situation. In Australia, the Army Ministry canceled special leaves indefinitely, and the government reached an accord with Pacific allies on defense plans, particularly of the Netherlands Indies, in the event of war. In Manila, the Philippine Cabinet requested immediate evacuation from Manila of all non-*

essential civilians (New York Times, Sunday, December 7, 1941).

Morning dawned bright and clear. Noumea harbor was calm. The crew prepared for this final leg of the South Pacific schedule. As they filed into the dispatch office for the pre-flight briefing, Folger Athearn, the Pan Am station manager, approached Bob Ford. "Bob, I've got an extra company passenger for you this morning."

"I guess we have plenty of room. Who is it?"

"Eugene Leach, our radio maintenance technician. He needs to get to Auckland to work on some radio equipment down there."

"Sure. Jack Poindexter will probably put him to work at the radio desk. He's been trying to get some relief ever since we had to shanghai him for the flight out of San Pedro!"

When Leach came aboard, Jack Poindexter greeted him like some long-lost brother. "Gene, glad to have you aboard!"

Leach shook Jack's hand and grinned. "Hey, glad to be on board. Noumea is okay, I guess, but I'm sure looking forward to a change of scenery for a while."

"If you like," Poindexter offered, "we can put you to work on our equipment while you're on board. How would you like to take the second watch after takeoff?"

"That'd be great. Is the gear still the same stuff we trained on at Treasure Island?"

"Hey, it's better," Poindexter assured him. "We've got new superhets installed since you came down here. And the new A-N homer feature is really slick. I'll give you a rundown on it when we're airborne."

Following a routine pre-flight inspection and start-up, NC18602 was airborne again; this time climbing out on the south-southeasterly heading to Auckland. When they reached cruising altitude, Poindexter demonstrated the new equipment for Leach.

"Look here, we just tune in any regular broadcast station," he explained, "get it identified and then switch to the A-N homer function. Then rotate the DF loop until the A and N signals blend into one continuous tone. That's the relative bearing to the station. Add in the plane's magnetic heading and you've got a good magnetic bearing to the station. Go ahead, try it."

Leach switched one of the receivers to the local broadcast band. Almost immediately he picked up the French-language station at Noumea. Interspersed with music were a number of announcements in French, most of which were beyond Leach's rudimentary knowledge of the language to interpret. When he switched on the A-N homer circuit, the high-pitched tone of the signals over-rode the broadcast sound. He experimented with the DF loop. He located the 'on course' bearing and found it to be extremely accurate.

"Jeez, that's sharp!" he exclaimed. "A guy could thread a needle with that kind of course guidance."

"That's the general idea. Why don't you just play with it for a while. Just be sure to keep the other receiver on our flight watch channel. Brown will give you the position reports to transmit." Poindexter nodded toward Rod Brown who was intently marking course and progress information on the navigation chart. "I'll be down in the galley if you need me."

For some time Leach experimented with the new equipment. He tuned in several stations, most of which were too weak to give accurate bearings. After a while he left the receiver tuned to the Noumea station and watched the tail bearing change as the aircraft's position changed. Soon, even the Noumea signal weakened. Finally, after about two hours of flight, it, too, was lost in the general static and noise of the broadcast band. He settled into the routine of guarding the operations frequency and sending the half-hourly position reports to the ground station. When they were about to pass ETP he decided to try the homing device again.

Hmm, he thought to himself, maybe we can pick up the Auckland broadcast now and try that homer gadget again. Once again, he slowly tuned across the AM broadcast band until he located an English-speaking station. Once again he switched on the A-N homer and watched as the bearing settled down to a narrowly defined course. Some two hours out of Auckland, Leach finally tired of experimenting with the new equipment and switched off the A-N homer circuit. As he did so, the voice of the Auckland announcer came in loud and clear.

"...no confirmation from the American Consulate in Auckland at this time, but it appears that Japanese naval forces have launched a surprise attack on the American naval base at Pearl Harbor on the Hawaiian Island of Oahu.

Unconfirmed reports indicate that at least two waves of bombers have destroyed or disabled a great number of naval vessels and have also attacked and severely damaged Army Air Force installations at Hickam Field and Schofield Barracks. We are attempting to obtain details from the American Consulate, but all communications are subject to priority delays. Please stand by and we will bring you the latest developments as they become available. Once again, repeating our initial report..."

"Jesus H. Christ!" Leach swore aloud. "That does it!"

"Gene, what's up?" Rod Brown asked as he heard Leach's exclamation.

"The Japs have attacked Pearl Harbor!" Leach blurted and stared at Brown with a slack expression, as if he could hardly believe what he had just heard.

"Hey, you've go to be kidding, right?" Brown chided him.

"No! No!" Leach insisted, "Just now... they bombed Pearl Harbor! No joke, man!"

Brown studied Leach's distressed expression. There was no doubting the urgency in his eyes. "You're sure about that?"

"Yeah... better tell Ford. We could be in a hellluva situation if they're invading Hawaii!"

The prospect of having their return flight to Hawaii intercepted by Japanese forces sent shivers up and down Brown's spine. Quickly he turned toward the cockpit and approached Bob Ford who was in the left seat.

"Skipper, I think we've got some bad news..." Brown was almost reluctant to say it.

Ford glanced toward his Second Officer. "Yeah, Rod, what is it?"

Brown took a deep breath. "Eugene Leach has intercepted a news report. The Japs have attacked Pearl Harbor!"

Ford turned slowly in his seat and looked at Brown. "You're sure about that? Better confirm it."

"Leach is still in contact with Noumea. Maybe he can get some more information."

Ford turned further and called to Eugene Leach across the flight deck to the radio desk. "Gene, get them to confirm that."

Suddenly Leach's headphones came alive with a call from FJPM, the Noumea ground station. The signal indicated that they had an urgent message for the ship. Leach transmitted the okay to go ahead and FJPM started pounding out the message in Morse Code:

PEARL HARBOR ATTACKED BY JAPANESE BOMBERS.IMPLEMENT PLAN A.

Leach transmitted a request for FJPM to repeat the message. As soon as the Noumea station repeated the message, Leach wrote it on a message pad and handed it to Ford.

Bob Ford, having lived with the possibility of this moment from the time they left San Francisco, knew instinctively what he had to do. Well, he thought to himself, now we'll find out what's in this envelope. He reached into the inside breast pocket of his uniform jacket and pulled out the legal-size envelope.

"Plan A – Top Secret – For Captain's Eyes Only"

He stared at the familiar letters for a moment. Then, slowly and carefully, tore open one end of the envelope and withdrew the document. There were three typewritten pages and a sheet of approach patterns.

Pan American Airways System
Pacific Division
Office of Division Manager

TOP SECRET   TOP SECRET   TOP SECRET

To: Captain, PAA Flight 6039 – SFO-LAX-HNL-CIS-SUV-NOU-AUK
    And return flight 6040.

From: Division Manager, Pacific Division

Subject: Special instructions to avoid hostile military activity.

I. Background

Pan American Airways, in cooperation with the Chief of Staff, United States Army, Commander-in-Chief, Pacific Fleet Operations, the Secretary of War, and the Secretary of State, has agreed to place its fleet of flying boats at the disposal of the military for whatever logistical or tactical purpose they may deem necessary at such time as hostilities break out between the United States forces and the military forces of the Imperial Japanese government.

In the event that you are required to open and read these instructions, you may assume that hostilities have already occurred and that the aircraft under your command represents a strategic military resource which must be protected and secured from falling into enemy hands.

Your operational scenario will be determined by the status of your flight at the time it becomes necessary to implement these instructions. Since it is not possible to foresee the exact time or place that hostilities will occur, the following alternatives have been developed for your flight route. Select the paragraph that most closely represents your en route status at such time as you are prepared to execute these instructions.

II. Action

If aircraft is moored at any en route station, cancel scheduled departure flight plan and consult with Pan American operations for further instructions. All ground station mangers have been provided with special instructions for securing aircraft and expediting diversionary operations.

1. En route LAX-HNL: Prior to ETP: Reverse course and divert to SFO. If past ETP, contact KVM to determine status of destination terminal. If possible, continue and land at HNL. If HNL is not open for arrival, divert to Hilo and await further instructions.

2. En Route HNL-CIS: Contact KVM or KCCG for instructions. Aircraft will either return to HNL or proceed to CIS and await further instructions.

3. En route CIS-SUV: Contact KCCG for instructions. Aircraft will either return to CIS or proceed to SUV and await further orders.

4. En route SUV-NOU: Contact Suva Radio or FJPM at Noumea. Aircraft will either return to Suva or proceed to NOU and await further orders.

5. En route NOU-AUK: Contact FJPM or Auckland Radio. Aircraft will either return to NOU or proceed to AUK and await further orders.

For the return portion of this flight, follow the above instructions in reverse order. In all cases, ONCE DIVERSION HAS BEEN EXECUTED, SHUT DOWN ALL RADIOS AND MAINTAIN STRICT RADIO SILENCE. AUTHENTICATION FLIGHT PATTERNS FOR NO-RADIO APPROACH AND LANDING AT EACH DIVERSION DESTINATION ARE LISTED IN THE APPENDIX TO THIS ORDER. ALL LINE STATION MANAGERS HAVE BEEN PROVIDED WITH DUPLICATE COPIES OF THESE PATTERNS AND WILL EXPECT YOU TO PROCEED IN ACCORDANCE THEREWITH. STRICT ADHERENCE TO AUTHENTICATION FLIGHT PATTERNS IS ESSENTIAL. ANY DEVIATION COULD RESULT IN AIRBORNE CHALLENGES BY MILITARY AIRCRAFT.

IMPORTANT: ONCE THESE INSTRUCTIONS HAVE BEEN EXECUTED, ALL OPERATIONAL INFORMATION REGARDING DISPOSITION AND PROGRESS OF YOUR FLIGHT SHALL BE CONSIDERED TOP SECRET. CREW MEMBERS SHALL BE INSTRUCTED TO SPEAK TO NO ONE REPEAT NO ONE OTHER THAN AUTHORIZED AND PROPERLY IDENTIFIED COMPANY OR MILITARY PERSONNEL WITH REGARD TO ACTIONS TAKEN OR PLANNED FOR THE FLIGHT. ANY BREACH OF THESE SECURITY MEASURES SHALL BE CONSIDERED A BREACH OF WARTIME SECURITY AND ANY PERSONNEL CREATING SUCH A BREACH OF SECURITY SHALL BE PROSECUTED UNDER THE WARTIME REGULATIONS CONCERNED WITH NATIONAL SECURITY MEASURES.

Ford stared at the document for a long moment, trying to digest the reality of the situation. Even though the possibility of war with Japan had been building in public awareness through newspaper and radio news reports that people heard every day, still, there seemed to be an air of unreality about it now that the moment had actually arrived. But Bob Ford was not one to ruminate too long on such things. His was a world of action and now he took the action required of him.

"Johnny, where's Steers?"

"He's on his break. Probably below having some lunch."

"Call down to the galley and have him come up here right away. Meanwhile, Gene, shut down that radio now! We're only a couple of hours out of Auckland and my guess is we'll be told to land there anyway. So we'll just do it. No telling if the Japs have any forces this far south, but if they do they could home in on our signals with no trouble at all. No point leading them in with us."

Then Ford reached into his flight case and brought out his personal .38 caliber revolver he habitually carried on all his flights. He strapped the holster around his waist and resumed his seat in the cockpit.

When Steers came up from the main cabin he had a puzzled expression on his face. "What's up? Barney said you wanted me up here right away. Anything wrong?"

"Only that the Japs have bombed Pearl Harbor!" Eugene Leach informed him.

"Holy shit! You're not kidding?"

"Nope. Just got the message from Noumea a few minutes ago."

Ford turned and called to Steers. "John, take up an observation post in the navigator's dome. Keep a sharp watch. If you so much as spot anything that doesn't look like a natural bird, holler. We don't know what the hell is out there right now."

"Yes, Sir!" Steers nodded and hastened to the rear of the flight deck where he passed through the hatchway to the cargo area and perched on the topmost rung of the navigator's ladder. Beyond the broad spread of the wings and the fuselage, all that was visible were scattered, puffy cumulus and a few wisps of higher cirrus clouds. The ocean below appeared deep blue and relatively calm from this altitude. Steers began a regular sweep of the horizon, not quite sure what he was looking for and wondering what Japanese warplanes would look like if any began to close in on the Boeing.

Ford then called Rod Brown forward from his navigator's table. "Rod, I'm not sure what we might have here in the way of a threat, but there's no sense in taking chances. Our direct route would be a logical search pattern for any enemy aircraft that might be in this area. Figure us a diversion – about fifty miles off course ought to do – and plot us a couple of headings for it."

"Okay, right away!" Brown returned to the chart table. In a couple of minutes he had a new heading which he posted on the instrument panel.

The remainder of the flight was conducted in almost total silence; each crew member pre-occupied with his own thoughts about the sudden turn of events. How would they get back to San Francisco? What were the chances of falling into Japanese hands? Was there any chance that the Japanese were attacking the Mainland U.S. as well? These and a hundred other unanswerable questions raced through their minds as they brought the big Boeing into Auckland Harbor.

Ford conferred with Johnny Mack as they studied the visual approach pattern spelled out on the last page of the Plan A document. A rather circuitous route was drawn over an outline of the harbor, with specific headings and altitudes. They would be required to head away from North Island for a pre-determined time, execute a formal procedure turn, make two other identifying turns approaching the coastline, and then take up a narrowly defined heading toward the landing channel in the harbor. There had to be no errors in executing this approach pattern. The New Zealand government was most likely on full alert by now. It was also most likely that fighter aircraft were already patrolling the perimeter of the island dominion to ward off any possible hostile intrusion. Ford and Mack studied the pattern intently and within a few minutes each knew exactly what he had to do. Ninety minutes after receiving news of the attack, NC18602 wheeled in toward the North Island coast, executed the designated flight patterns and landed without incident.

Upon coming ashore, Ford was greeted by Bill Mullahey, the Pan American station manager. "Boy, are we glad to see you!" Mullahey exclaimed as he shook Bob Ford's hand. "We've been trying to contact you by radio for the past two hours. Didn't know if you'd been shot down somewhere, or had turned back to Noumea, or what..."

"When we got that message from Noumea and after opening the Plan A letter, I decided to shut down the radios right then. I figured there was nowhere else to go except to come in. So, what do we do now?"

"Our instructions are to wait for orders from the Company. There's only one hitch to that, though," Mullahey began to explain.

"Yeah? What's that?"

"All point-to-point communications have been put on a restricted schedule. The only messages getting in or out have to go through the coding office at the American Consulate. Right now they're so swamped we don't know how soon they'll be able to get our messages processed. It could be several hours; it could be several days."

"What are we supposed to do in the meantime? Just sit around and twiddle our thumbs?" Ford remonstrated.

"Looks that way, Bob." Mullahey shrugged. "Our orders are not to make a move until we hear from New York headquarters. The best I can suggest is that you haunt the American Consulate office until they come up with something for us. But it could be a long wait."

When the crew had been bussed to the Grand Hotel in Auckland and checked in, Ford went immediately to the American Consulate. The message center was a scene of hectic and confused activity as couriers and clerks attempted to keep up with the rapid flow of news and messages. Everything was in diplomatic code and had to be decoded before proper delivery could be made to the addressees. He could do nothing but wait for the harried code clerks to uncover the message he was waiting for.

NC18602 in the harbor at Auckland, NZ

CHAPTER VI
WESTWARD HO!

One week after landing at Auckland, Bob Ford and his crew were still waiting for instructions from Company headquarters. They had fallen into a daily routine of sleeping, eating, and strolling the streets of the city while Ford haunted the American Consulate message center for any word regarding their next move. The heavy flow of radio messages coming into the Consulate's communications office kept piling up as the code clerks went through the laboriously slow task of decoding and delivering them.

This particular morning, December 14th, Ford had arrived, as usual, at the Consulate office just after breakfast. He was standing in front of a large bulletin board, reading some of the latest news dispatches that had been cleared for public consumption. Nowhere in this display of war news did there seem to be any encouraging word: Manila and Wake Island were under attack; Midway and Guam had been badly mauled and barely hanging on; and Canton Island – the key refueling point for their return flight – had been evacuated. It seemed as though they were caught in an ever-tightening noose. What possible course of action could they take to get the Clipper home safely? Ford reviewed a dozen possibilities in his mind. But he knew he could not execute any of them without confirmation from the Company. Would their plans agree with his own ideas? Would they even have a plan that was feasible? From 10,000 miles away in New York City, how could they know the best course of action? And, damnit, what was taking them so long in getting the orders delivered? Ordinarily, Bob Ford was a very patient, methodical professional; but these last few days of waiting had pushed him very close to the limits of his patience.

"Captain Ford?" the Consulate officer called, as he approached him.

Ford turned away from the news board and saw the clerk carrying several message forms in his hand. "Yes, I'm Ford. Do you have something for me?"

"Yes – finally, sir – sorry for all the delay, but you know," the clerk was apologetic, "it's been a real mess. But I think we have what you have been waiting for. Would you mind signing this receipt book?" The clerk shoved forward the open ledger and a pen.

Ford signed the book and handed it back. The clerk, in turn, handed him one of the message forms. "Thank you, sir," he said, then returned to the code room.

Ford walked slowly over to a chair against the wall, sat down, unfolded the message and began to read it.

SECURITY: TOP SECRET

TO   : CAPTAIN ROBERT FORD

FROM   : CHIEF, FLIGHT OPERATIONS
         PAN AMERICAN AIRWAYS SYSTEM
         CHRYSLER BUILDING
         NEW YORK CITY, NY

SUBJECT : DIVERSION PLANS FOR NC18602

NORMAL RETURN ROUTE CANCELED STOP PROCEED AS FOLLOWS COLON STRIP ALL COMPANY MARKINGS COMMA REGISTRATION NUMBERS COMMA AND IDENTIFIABLE INSIGNIA FROM EXTERIOR SURFACES STOP PROCEED WESTBOUND SOONEST YOUR DISCRETION TO AVOID HOSTILITIES AND DELIVER NC18602 TO MARINE TERMINAL LAGUARDIA FIELD NEW YORK STOP GOOD LUCK STOP

Good luck, hell! Ford thought, we're going to need miracles, not luck. He folded the message and stuffed it in his pocket. Then he hurried to the Pan American operations office to confer with Bill Mullahey.

Mullahey frowned as he contemplated the message form that Ford had handed him. "They don't expect much, do they?" he muttered sarcastically. "Just head out like it was a Sunday drive or something! Christ, Bob, this is survey flight time all over again. Talk about carts before horses, this is the prize example!"

Ford tried to sound a reasonable note, "They're right about one thing: we can't go back the way we came. And we can't just sit here and wait for the Japs to take over. Looks like we don't have much choice."

"Yeah, you're probably right." Mullahey paused. "...Well, I guess it's back to school time – and we'd better get that geography lesson going! What do you have on board in the way of charts?"

"Just the usual Mercators for the normal route. They overlap a little in a westerly direction, but not enough to even get us to Australia, let alone clear to New York. We're going to have to come up with some other sources."

Mullahey thought for a moment. "I think I know where I can get some geography text books and atlases and possibly some marine charts – from the Auckland library. Meanwhile I think we'd better get some of the crew down here to help my boys strip those marking off the ship."

Ford nodded assent to these suggestions. Then they both got into Mullahey's car and drove to the Grand Hotel. It was noon as they arrived, and they found all the crew in the dining room having lunch.

"Eat fast, boys. We've got our orders and there's a job to do," Ford declared as he approached their table.

"Well, it's about time!" John Steers exclaimed. "What's the word?"

"First order of business is we've got to strip off all Company insignia and registration markings from the ship. Bill here needs you to help his ground crew to do that. Meanwhile we need to figure out a way home. The New York office wants us to head west and get back to New York the long way 'round."

"Christ, Skipper," Rod Brown reacted, "that's a helluva route. Where the hell are we supposed to get gas and service? And we don't even have nav charts beyond Auckland."

"Yeah, I know," Ford agreed, "but it looks as though that's about the only way we can go without running into the Japs. Bill thinks we can find some maps to figure some kind of route. Johnny, you and Rod come with us and we can all work on this flight problem. Meanwhile, the rest of you get down to the ship and help with the paint stripping. Swede," and here he turned to Swede Rothe, "you and Parrish get moving on refueling. And top those tanks with as much as our takeoff weight will allow. No telling how or where we'll be able to get aviation fuel... We'll have to see how this flight route works out."

After a hurried gulping down of food and drink, they were all driven to the harbor in the crew limousine that Bill Mullahey had ordered. Once there, they met with Verne White, Pan Am's chief mechanic at Auckland, and together with his maintenance crew, began stripping the paint markings from the flying boat.

Meanwhile Mullahey drove Bob Ford, Johnny Mack, and Rod Brown to the Auckland Public Library where they explained their needs to the librarian. Shortly they were huddled around a table with a mass of old marine charts, atlases, and schoolboy geography books, looking for the best way home.

"Look here," Brown pointed to a double-page illustration of a world map in a school geography book. "The hop to Australia should be no problem. We can head for Sydney or Brisbane and then from there to someplace on the west coast. But then we've got the problem of getting across the Indian Ocean. A direct route to Africa looks as though it would be too long for our best long-range cruise endurance."

"Well," Johnny Mack suggested, "what about cutting across northwest up toward Indo-China? Maybe hit Darwin and then keep in close to the coast via Java and India?"

"That would put us closer to any possible Jap military action." Brown replied.

"Yeah, but there sure as hell ain't no refueling stations in the middle of the Indian Ocean!"

"I think Johnny's got a point." Ford broke in. "It's going to be a trade-off either way. Either we load to the gills and hope the headwinds don't slow us down too much for a direct run to Africa, or we take a chance that we can get gas at some of those ports up toward Java and India without running into any shooting. Considering that we have zero weather info from here on out, I'd say our best bet is toward the northwest. Once we get across India and Arabia to Africa we should be pretty much home free. We'd be back in Company territory if we can reach Leopoldville[5]."

---

[5] Present-day Kinshasa, Zaire

The four of them were silent then; each studying the charts laid our before them and trying to visualize the best possible route home. Very soon they had a consensus.

"We're agreed then." Ford summarized their decision. "From here to Brisbane, then up to Darwin. Darwin to Surabaya, Surabaya to Trincomalee[6], then to Karachi, Bahrain, Khartoum, and Leopoldville. Once we reach Leopoldville we're back at Company facilities and it should be no big problem outfitting for the run to Natal, then north via Port of Spain to LaGuardia. Any questions?"

"How about gas and oil and food provisions?" Brown asked.

"We're just going to have to take our chances. Maybe Bill can try to get word ahead through the consulate channels to those locations and they can arrange for supplies through local military sources. I'm sure by now the Brits have increased mobilization across that whole southern region. Should include plenty of aviation action and they ought to have the 100 octane we'll need. As for food," Ford paused, "we just may have to do a little shopping... Can we get some cash advance to cover that, Bill?" he turned and asked Bill Mullahey.

"I'll give you what I can from our cash fund here, but it's not much. We may have to have the Company wire funds ahead for you. I'll see what I can do."

Ford nodded and then turned his attention once again to the maps spread out before him. "Rod, take these charts and see what sort of navigation sense you can make out of them. We'll need some approximate course lines and DR headings. Without any weather or winds aloft data we're really going to be flying blind as far as ground progress is concerned. Let's just assume it'll be headwinds all the way. That way we can keep our reserve requirements on the conservative side."

"Sure, Skipper," Brown responded, as he studied the charts and measured distances and headings in his mind's eye. "I think I can run true course line interpolations on the back side of our regular charts and expand each leg depiction that way. Our copy of Bowdich's Navigation ought to give us good approximations on the magnetic variations as we go along."

"Okay, if we're all agreed, let's get on with it," Ford concluded. "Now let's head back to the dock and see how that paint stripping job is coming."

---

[6] British naval station in Ceylon – today's Sri Lanka

Shortly after they returned to the harbor, a courier in a United States Consulate car drove up to the Pan American operations office. He walked quickly over to Bill Mullahey.

"Mr. Mullahey, I have another dispatch for Captain Ford. Is he available to sign for it?"

Mullahey nodded at the courier. "Yeah, he's down at the dock. Come on, I'll take you down there."

The two men left the operations office and walked down the path to the dock where NC18602 was being stripped of its markings. Ford and Chief Mechanic Verne White were standing on the dock supervising the operation.

"Bob," Mullahey called as they approached, "here's another dispatch for you from the Consulate."

Ford turned as the two men came down the ramp. The courier had him sign the receipt book again and handed him the new message. He studied it briefly before commenting. "Well, that'll change our plans a bit," he thought aloud.

"How's that, Bob?" Mullahey asked.

"It looks like we've got to do some backtracking. Now the Company wants us to return to Noumea as soon as possible and evacuate all Pan American personnel and their families to Gladstone, Australia. They say they've arranged for ground transport for them from there to Sydney where they'll be shipped back to the States via surface transport. Also," and here he turned to Verne White, "Verne, looks like you'll be coming with us!"

"The hell, you say!" White exclaimed. "How come?"

"Seems like they have a special assignment for you at Karachi. And a couple of the Noumea mechanics are being reassigned to some airbase in Bahrain. Looks like we're all in this together from now on. After that we'll be on our own getting back to New York."

"That'll revise your initial flight route, but it shouldn't change the overall plan by much," Mullahey reasoned.

"Yeah, I guess so, but there is one other thing... You have a couple of spare engines stored here, don't you?"

"Right," Verne White answered. "What about 'em?"

"Company says we need to tear them down and stow them aboard for spare parts. Can we get that done and be ready in time to head out tomorrow?"

White thought a moment. "If we knock off the paint stripping job and get all hands to tearing down those engines, we might get the

70

job done by late tomorrow. You're the Captain... what priority do you want to assign on this?"

Ford turned and looked over the Boeing rocking quietly at the dock. The flight and ground crew members were busy scraping and removing the paint markings. Most of the job was done except for a large American flag on top of the wing. What the hell, Ford thought, that's good enough. Those engine parts are going to be more important than some paint marks. "Let's knock off the paint job and get on those engines," he decided. Then he turned to Mullahey. "Oh, and while I think of it, Bill, speaking of personnel transfers, we'd better plan on having Eugene Leach stay with us. Just in case we need maintenance help with the radios. I'll authorize his assignment as a crew member."

They immediately called the flight and ground crew members off the paint stripping job and set them to work tearing down the two Wright Cyclone engines that had been part of the spare parts inventory of the Auckland base. It was no simple task. The 14 cylinders of each engine were configured in two radial rows of seven cylinders each, plus the accessory sections containing the oil and gas line connections, electrical connections, along with the propellers, hubs, and prop governor controls. Each cylinder was held down by 16 tightly-secured head bolts that had to be unscrewed with great care to avoid stripping the threads. Verne White, along with Swede Rothe and Jocko Parrish, supervised the operation as they instructed the maintenance crew and the flight crew members in the delicate art of dismantling these complex power plants.

They worked through the night and into the early hours of the next morning. By 3 A.M they had managed to fully dismantle only one of the engines. The parts had been carefully stowed in various passenger compartments, distributed so as to keep the weight and balance as close to normal as possible.

"Hell, that's enough for now," Ford exclaimed. "Let's knock off and get a little shut-eye. We can get going on the other engine later in the morning."

The crew was more than happy to agree with their Captain. It had been a long and grueling day. Bleary-eyed and grimy, they all piled into the crew limo and were taken to the hotel for a few hours of welcomed rest."

"Sleep fast, guys!" Ford quipped. "The morning call will be 7 A.M."

All too soon, after only four hours of rest, they once again went to work dismantling the second engine. They worked through the morning and afternoon and stowed the last of the dismantled power plant on board by 7 P.M. But any thought of the crew returning to the hotel again for a night's sleep was quickly dispelled by Ford's next order.

"Everyone grab a bunk or seat on board and get what shut-eye you can right here. We have to arrive at Noumea early enough in the morning to give those people time to pack and get on board. We can't radio our intentions because of the aircraft communications blackout and we can't risk visual detection by any Jap patrols that might be in the area. So we're aiming for a night takeoff around 10 P.M. That should put us into Noumea around dawn and we'll still have time to load and get out of there for the flight to Gladstone. Any questions?"

There were none. Twelve weary and oil-stained crew members climbed aboard the Boeing. Each sought out a bunk or double seat to crawl into. Lulled by the gentle rocking motion of the big ship, each of them soon fell into various stages of sleep or dozing, hoping to restore their energy for the ordeal that lay ahead of them. It would begin in a little less than three hours.

Bill Mullahey peered into the darkness ahead of the small boat. Except for the electric lantern he held in his hand, no lights were visible along the length of the seaplane channel. As he motored slowly along the length of the takeoff area he strained to detect the presence of any floating object that might present a risk for the takeoff. Water takeoffs and landings at night were marginally safe at best. Under these conditions the risk was magnified many times. With full fuel tanks and the added weight of the stripped down engines, NC18602 was at least 1,000 pounds over-grossed. Ford would need every bit of takeoff length to break free of the calm water of the bay. There would be no room for error. As Mullahey approached the far end of the channel, with his electric lantern providing the only visual reference, he slowed to a stop and took one more look around. Then, very carefully and deliberately, he held the lantern aloft and waved it in a horizontal arc toward the takeoff end of the channel where Ford waited with engines idling.

"There it is," Johnny Mack called out. "Bill's reached the end of the channel. That's the 'all clear for takeoff' signal."

Bob Ford had also spotted the light signal. He tightened his grip on the throttle controls. "Okay, Swede, full power follow through, now!"

Once again the overpowering roar of the four Wright Cyclone engines filled the cabin. NC18602 surged forward into the blackness, guided only by the dim point of light at the far end of the channel. Within 35 seconds, Ford had the big ship on the step and, with a gentle back pressure on the yoke, broke free of the water and settled into a shallow climb. As they reached 200 feet, they passed the motor launch where Bill Mullahey was still waving his lantern.

"Godspeed, you guys!" Mullahey uttered a quiet prayer as the Boeing roared past. "...and good luck. You're going to need it!"

ITE	AIRCRAFT	DEP. POINT	ACC. POINT	FLITE TIME	REMARKS
EC 41	N18606	SFO-SN PEDRO-HNL		22 HRS 58 MIN	
EC 41	N18602	HONOLULU	CANTON IS.	12 HRS 57 MIN	
41	"	CANTON IS.	SUVA, FIJI	8 HRS 38 MIN	
EC 41	"	SUVA	NOUMEA	6 HRS 13 MIN	OVER NITE ACCOMODATIONS NOUMEA ABOARD FORMER CURTIS PUBLISHING CO. YATC
41	"	NOUMEA	AUCKLAND	7 HRS 43 MIN	RADIO OPERATOR, LISTENING ... TO PRESS DISPATCHES, INTERCEPTED NEWS OF PEARL HARBOR ATTA...
? 41	"	AUCKLAND	NOUMEA	8 HRS. 10 MIN	PURPOSE OF THIS FLITE, TO EV... PAA PERSONNEL AND DEPEN...
C 41	"	NOUMEA	GLADSTONE AUSTRALIA	6 HRS 36 MIN	EVACUEES SENT TO SYDNEY... LATER HOME TO US, BY BOAT... STAT. MECHS CONTINUED WITH US... WAS LEFT IN KARACHI, THE OTH... IN BAHRAIN, TO SET UP MAINT...
DEC 41	"	GLADSTONE	DARWIN	11 HRS 11 MIN	
DEC 41	"	DARWIN	SURABAYA	8 HRS. 41 MIN	
DEC 41	"	SURABAYA	TRINCOMALEE	20 HRS. 26 MIN	
C 41	"	TRINCOMALEE	TRINCOMALEE	1 HR. 09 MIN	CYLINDER FAILURE #3 ENGINE.
C 41	"	TRINCOMALEE	KARACHI	9 HRS 40 MIN	
EC 41	"	KARACHI	BAHRAIN	8 HRS 09 MIN	ETC
C 41	"	BAHRAIN	KHARTOUM	11 HRS 16 MIN	PASSED OVER MECCA, PILGRIMAGE IN PROC...
V 42	"	KHARTOUM	LEOPOLDVILLE	10 HRS 23 MIN	LANDED IN CONGO RIVER
N 42	"	LEOPOLDVILLE	NATAL	23 HRS 35 MIN	LANDED NATAL WITH APPROX. 2 HRS RES...
J 42	"	NATAL	TRINIDAD	13 HRS 52 MIN	
IN 42	"	TRINIDAD	NEW YORK	15 HRS 46 MIN	TOTAL FLYING TIME ACCORDING TO LOGBOOK 269 HRS, 22 MIN.

4th Officer John Steer's Flight Log

MONTH OF DECEMBER 1941

Date	AIRCRAFT FLOWN			CROSS COUNTRY		REMARKS	Aircraft Classification		Hood	Instrument	Trainer	Day	Night
3/8	BOEING 314 #18602			SFO	HNL	Schedule Tr. # 6030	5 M water			1:20			7:00
4/5	"			HNL	CNM					1:00			2:4
5	"			CNM	SUV								
4/7	"			SUV	NOU								
7	"			NOU	AUK					:30			
15	"			AUK	NOU	FERRY				:30			7:4
15	"			NOUMEA	GLADSTONE AUST	"							
16/17	"			GLADSTONE	DARWIN AUST	"							
17/18	"			DARWIN	SURABAYA JAVA	"							
2/22	"			SURABAYA	TRINCOMALEE CEYLON					1:00			15:30
24	"			TRINCOMALEE	TRINCOMALEE, TURNAROUND OFF ENGINE FAIL								
26	"			TRINCOMALEE	KARACHI INDIA	FERRY							2:4
28	"			KARACHI	BEHREIN AR	"							
28	"			BAHREIN	KHARTOUM SUDAN	"							2:3

CERTIFIED CORRECT	PILOT'S SIGNATURE		
	Jn. L. Mack	Page Total PAA / Brought Forward / Total to Date	138.52 118.52 / 1583:57 757.44 / 1722:48 874:36

TOTAL SOLO			
Solo Page Total	138:58	Page T
Solo Brought Fwd	2134:26	Total
Solo Total	2273:24	TOTA

1st Officer John Mack's Flight Log

CHAPTER VII
RETURN TO NOUMEA

Bud Washer, one of Pan Am's mechanics at the Noumea base, rolled over on his right side and glanced at the clock on the night stand beside the bed. 6 A.M., December 16th. His wife stirred in her sleep but did not waken. The stillness of dawn was broken only by the distant calls of a flock of mynah birds in the palm trees outside the compound. Bud closed his eyes again. Just a few more minutes, he thought; nothing to rush for this morning. And he dozed off again.

The sound began as a low hum. Very quickly it grew loud enough to mask the distant squawking of the birds. It penetrated Washer's sleep-drugged mind and he woke again, suddenly, as the hum became a roar and he recognized it as the sound of a high-powered aircraft coming in very low and very fast. "Christ! What the hell is that?" he exclaimed, as he jumped from the bed and ran to the window.

His wife rolled over, propped herself on one elbow and brushed her hair away from her eyes. "Bud, what is it? Is something wrong?"

"I dunno," he responded, still only half awake. "Might be a Jap air raid!" Something real big just passed over the house. Wait a minute..."

"Oh, God! What'll we do?"

Bud crouched down low at the window sill and drew his wife down beside him. "Wait a minute, wait a minute..." He tried to calm her as he peered out at the grey dawn and attempted to make out the identity of the intruder that had passed overhead. Then, within a couple of seconds, he recognized the rapidly receding shape as it headed toward the harbor. "Hell, that's the Boeing... The Clipper, probably coming back from Auckland. But what's it doing coming in this time of day? We didn't have any word on a return flight schedule. I'd better high-tail it down to operations. This could be important."

The Washers were not the only ones rudely awakened by the roar of the engines as NC18602 came in low over the town and circled to land in the harbor. Folger Athearn, the station manager, along with everyone else in the sleepy community, had responded in one way or another to the sudden wake-up call. When it was quickly determined that it was not a Japanese air raid, most of them ran down to the harbor dock to greet the unexpected arrival.

Bob Ford stepped down from his cockpit seat, stretched and moved to the middle of the flight deck while the docking crew warped the Boeing alongside the ramp and set the gangway in place. "Listen up, everyone," he addressed the crew as they secured their respective operating positions. "Everyone stays either on the ship or just on the dock. I'm going up to operations to confer with the station manager, but I want the rest of you to stick close here. We're getting out of here as fast as we can so we can get to Gladstone with some daylight left. Swede, get those tanks topped and check those engines very carefully. From here on out it's a poker game for sure."

The operations office was crowded with company personnel and their families, all wondering what this sudden, unannounced arrival meant. Folger Athearn emerged from his office, followed by Bob Ford. He raised his arms and waved to get everyone's attention. "Quiet, people! Captain Ford has something to say... Quiet please!"

A hush came over the office as Bob Ford came forward. "As all of you are probably aware, there's no way we can make the return flight to Honolulu. I have orders from the Company to take NC02 westbound and try to get it to New York.."

A murmur of surprise and questioning ran through the assembled crowd. Ford waved for silence again.

"But we can't take all of you that far. Mechanics Bud Washer and Ralph Hitchcock will be coming with us to help maintain our engines and report to new assignments at Bahrain. All other employees and families will fly with us as far as Gladstone, Australia. From there you will be taken by train or bus to Sydney and loaded on a passenger liner that will take you home to the States."

"You mean we're evacuating everyone?"

"Yes... All personnel and their families."

"When do we leave?"

"In one hour."

A loud buzz of response again arose in the crowded office. "One hour! Hell, we can't get our belongings together that quick! Can't we have more time?"

"I'm afraid not," Ford explained, "We have to reach Gladstone before dark. As for your belongings, with a full load of fuel and the spare engine parts on board, the additional weight of passengers and luggage will have to be kept to a minimum. Only one suitcase for each employee and family member. Everything else gets left behind!"

The prospect of leaving all of their accumulated belongings behind except for one suitcase apiece sent a loud murmur of protest through the crowd. But they all quickly realized that their options were very limited. With a few more words from the station manager, they were sent home to pack and told to report to the operations office within the deadline.

Meanwhile, there was one more piece of unfinished loading that had to be taken care of. In addition to the spare engine parts loaded on at Auckland, Pan American had ordered that another engine, still stored in its shipping crate as part of the spare parts inventory of the Noumea base, was to be taken on board and flown to Karachi, India. There, it was to be off-loaded and made part of the spare parts inventory of a newly opened Allied military airbase. Swede Rothe and John Parrish supervised the loading of this bulky, heavy package. It was not an easy task. They opened the navigator's hatch on top of the fuselage. This led to the cargo compartment directly behind the flight deck. A dockside crane gingerly lifted the crated engine and it was lowered carefully into the cargo area. It cleared the sides of the opening by inches. Then it was tied down securely with tie-down ropes along with a spare drum of engine oil.

When the engine loading was completed, all the employees and their families came aboard. With all fuel tanks topped, NC18602 was now at a gross weight far higher than the limits calculated by Boeing's design engineers. Ford knew that climb out after takeoff would be slow and shallow. He taxied the ship to the extreme eastern end of the harbor and pointed its bow westward toward the open sea. Once again throttles went forward, engines roared, spray whipped over the sea wings and, after what seemed like an eternity but was only a few seconds over the maximum allowable time at full power, the Clipper lifted off the water. The journey into the unknown had begun.

Johnny Mack looked down at the dark blue sea as they approached the Australian coast. It looks the same here as it does approaching Hawaii, he thought. Soon the dark blue turned to a lighter blue and finally the color turned to brilliant aquamarine as they crossed the Great Barrier Reef and approached Heron Island. Gladstone lay just beyond.

"Johnny," Ford call to him, "Let's circle that channel between the mainland and that large island just north of the harbor. It looks like the most likely place to set down. Get on down to about 500 feet and we'll drag it both ways for wind check and debris."

Mack nodded. "Okay, Skipper," and he backed off his throttles.

The Boeing settled into a shallow descent. They flew over the town, circled north and let down to 500 feet to inspect the landing area. When they had satisfied themselves that the area was clear, Ford lined up on a final approach that was as close into the wind as possible. He came into the final landing attitude and eased down for the moment of contact. Touchdown was so smooth that, had it not been for the sound of the water slapping against the hull, the passengers might have thought they were still airborne.

Taxiing back toward the town's dock area, Ford searched for a suitable anchorage. Suddenly he spotted a lone motor launch coming toward them. The one occupant was waving a large white flag.

"Looks like he's waving us in. Should we follow him?" Johnny Mack asked.

"Might as well... But watch for shallows. I don't want this ship hung up on a sandbar or reef."

They followed the launch in toward an area where there was a low floating dock. The launch circled in toward the dock, then came back toward them and stopped at a small buoy just offshore. He apparently wanted them to tie up there.

"Shut down Two and Three," Ford called to Swede Rothe. "Steers, Parrish, man the bow hatch and stand by to snag that buoy."

With the inboard engines shut down, Ford jockeyed the flying boat toward the buoy. John Steers, in the bow hatch, reached out with his boat hook, snagged the line and dropped it over the bow post.

"All engines off!" Ford called. "Switches off."

As soon as all stations were secured, Ford went below to the main lounge. He opened the hatch and stepped out on the sea wing as the motor launch approached.

"Ahoy! Are you Captain Ford?" the figure in the boat called.

"Yes. Can you tow us into the dock?"

"Yes, I think so. Just let me get a line on your tail hook. My men on the dock can warp you in," he said, waving to a small group of people standing on the floating pier. Very shortly NC18602 was tied up to the dock and a makeshift gangway of broad planks spanned the short distance between the sea wing and the dock. Ford was first off and strode over to greet the man from the motor launch as he tied up and came ashore.

"I didn't expect anyone to know me by name," he said as he extended his hand.

"Jeff Willoughby at yer service, mate." The young man in the khaki shorts and shirt introduced himself. "We got a message from your embassy in Canberra just last night. Said to expect you blokes and a few of your company people. Understand they're to be transported to Sydney to catch a steamer for San Francisco."

"Yes, that's right," Ford nodded. "I'm glad to see that at least some communications are working. Do you have transportation available for them?"

"Yes, sir. They can stay the night in town and then we'll get 'em boarded on the train first thing in the morning."

"Good. Now, can we get any 100 octane aviation gas for the plane? We need to fuel up and get out of here at first light for Darwin."

"Blimey, Captain, I dunno about 100 octane. We can check around town, but I couldn't say as how they have any of that in these parts," Willoughby replied.

"If it's okay with you, I'll send a couple of my crew members into town to check it out. Meanwhile if you'd give my passengers a hand at unloading, I'm sure they'd appreciate it."

Willoughby agreed and immediately signaled for some of the men standing on the dock to assist the passengers. Soon the passengers were all on board the busses. Meanwhile Ford went back to the ship and briefed the crew and the mechanics from Auckland and Noumea who were still on board.

"Johnny, you and Swede go into town and check around to see if you can locate any aviation fuel. The rest of us will bunk down right here aboard ship. We want to get an early start out of here in the morning."

After a fruitless search, Rothe and Mack reported back, "Sorry to report, Captain," Rothe said, "but there's not a drop of 100 octane to be had. It's either take a chance on using auto gas or try to make it to Darwin on what we have left in the tanks right now."

"How was our fuel level when we shut down?"

"Both main tanks are down one third each. The sea wing tanks about the same. I figure we should be okay to continue on to Darwin if we don't tangle with too much headwind."

"Then Darwin it is," Ford decided. "Just hope they have the 100 octane there."

There was just one more thing to take care of, Ford remembered, as they returned to the ship. How would they pay for the fuel, food, and other services they would require from here on? With no Pan American bases to support them, Ford knew that they would be paying their own way at every stop. And they had very little money. Most of their personal funds had been spent on food and lodging at Auckland during the long wait for instructions. No one had anticipated, when they left San Francisco, that they would have to be on their own for such a long time. Something had to be arranged, or they might find themselves stranded somewhere with no way to get home.

"Jeff," Ford turned to Jeff Willoughby as they stood on the dock, "did that message from the embassy say anything about how we were to arrange payment for our gas and other services from here on out?"

"Can't say as how it did, Captain. Only that you'd be authorized to buy what you needed. Just keep a record of all expenses and they'd take care of it at the far end."

"That may be easy for them to say. We spent most of our cash just for lodging and food while waiting in Auckland. We're all just about flat broke. Is there any way we can get a cash advance... say, sign for it here, keep all receipts and the Company will take care of it later?"

Willoughby thought on the matter for some moments. Then, "Well, Captain, I'm not sure but what the higher-ups might take a mite unkindly to me opening the company safe on such short notice, but I think I could manage to find a bit of cash for you. Come on with me up to the office and we'll have a look-see."

Willoughby managed to come up with five hundred dollars in United States currency.

80

"That's mighty generous of you, Jeff," Ford said, as he took the cash. "We'll be sure to keep all receipts and I'll make sure that Pan Am accounting gets this back to you pronto after we get to New York."

Ford shook Jeff Willoughby's hand. "Thanks for all your help."

"Just you blokes get that big flyin' machine back safe and yourselves safe with it. Maybe we'll see you again some time."

"Count on it!"

Ford and his crew bunked down on the Boeing to grab what sleep they could before the early morning departure into more unknown territory.

Clipper Names & Aircraft Specifications

BOEING 314

NC18601 Honolulu Clipper
NC18602 California Clipper (renamed Pacific Clipper)
NC18603 Yankee Clipper
NC18604 Atlantic Clipper
NC18605 Dixie Clipper
NC18606 American Clipper

BOEING 314A

NC18609 Pacific Clipper
NC18611 Anzac Clipper
NC18612 Capetown Clipper

Development: The Model 314 was a combination of the Wellwood E. Beall's design and the Boeing XB-15 bomber.
The aircraft first flew on June 7, 1938. A total of 12 aircraft were built of which, the last one was retired in 1951.
Modifications: Model A314 – upgraded engines and increased fuel capacity; Six aircraft built to this configuration. (3 to BOAC).
Crew: 6-10
Wingspan: 152 feet / 46.3 m
Wingarea: 2867.0 square feet / 266.3 square meters
Length: 106 feet / 32.3 m
Height: 28 feet / 8.4 m
Gross Weight: 82,500 lbs / 37,414 kg
Empty Weight: 50,268 lbs / 22,797 kg
Engines: 4x Wright GR-2600-A2 "Double Cyclone" 14-cylinder air-cooled Radial Engines (1600 horsepower each)
Maximum Speed: 193 mph / 311 km/h / 167 kt
Cruise Speed: 183 mph / 294 km/h / 158 kt
Cruise Ceiling: 13,400 feet / 4085 m
Maximum Ceiling: 19,600 feet / 6030 m
Climb: 565 ft/min / 172 m/min
Range: 3500 miles / 5635 km
Payload: 40-74 (36 night) passengers

CHAPTER VIII
THE DARK SIDE OF THE MOON

The next morning Ford inspected all the passenger compartments to be sure that all the spare parts were securely tied down. Forward, in the galley, Barney Sawicki and Verne Edwards were busy stowing what food and supplies they had been able to find in the town. Barney looked up and greeted Ford as he came forward. "It won't be the gourmet fare we carried out of San Francisco, but I guess it'll stick to your ribs well enough until we get to a Company base."

"Fine, Barn," Ford grinned. "Just so it'll keep the hungries away," as he turned and strode up the stairwell to the flight deck.

Rod Brown and Jim Henricksen were huddled together over the navigator's table, studying the makeshift charts and geography books that were going to serve as their only navigational references. Jack Poindexter was seated at the radio desk; but there was not much that he had to do. They would be flying in total radio silence, so there was no need to ground check the transmitters. He idly tuned the receivers to see if he could pick up any broadcast of war news, but reception was noisy and he could not find a clear signal anywhere. Swede Rothe and John Parrish were carefully calculating their expected fuel consumption. With the tanks only two-thirds full, they would have to find the most effective mixture, r.p.m., and manifold pressure settings that would assure them of sufficient range to make it to Darwin. With no place to land a flying boat in this continent of scrub land, desert, mountains, and rain forest, it was going to be an all-or-nothing flight: one long leg of about eleven hours.

"Rod," Bob Ford came up the stairwell and called to Rod Brown, "I've got a little project for you."

Brown turned from the chart table. "Oh, what's that?"

"Take this envelope. It's got five hundred cash that Jeff Willoughby dug up for us. Put it in the safe under the navigator's table. I want you to keep accounts of where and how we spend it. Make some kind of file for all our receipts. We'll need detailed documentation on what we spend it on, where, and how much. We'll turn it in to accounting when we get home."

Brown took the envelope containing the cash and turned it over in his hands. "You sure this is going to be enough?"

"It's going to have to be enough. At least until we can reach the Company base at Leopoldville. Just be sure to keep complete records. Accounting can get might fussy about audit trails before they'll pay up."

Brown opened the safe and placed the envelope inside. Then he carefully closed and locked it.

"Okay, listen up everyone." Ford addressed the assembled crew, "From here on out we might as well be exploring the dark side of the moon. I expect we'll be doing more 'seat of the pants' flying than any of us has ever done before. So let's run a tight watch on the flight deck, get your duty rotations in order and stay alert. We'll be observing complete radio silence and any night flying will be done with all navigation lights off. Jack," and here he turned toward Jack Poindexter at the radio desk, "I know this will probably be a very boring radio watch, but just monitor the receivers for any bit of info you might be able to pick up."

"Aye, Skipper," Poindexter agreed, "it'll be a chance thing if we pick up anything. We don't have frequency charts for this part of the world. But I'll tune across the different bands. Maybe we'll get lucky and find a good international short wave broadcast."

"Let's hope so. Anyone have any questions? If not, let's fly!"

Once again the familiar litany of pre-flight checks, engine starts, and instrument checks dominated the atmosphere of the flight deck as the four Wright engines came alive. The triple vertical stabilizers of the tail assembly trembled as NC18602 strained at the mooring lines. In short order those lines were released and the big boat moved away from the floating dock and into the channel. After a quick check for floating debris, Ford turned into the wind and pushed the throttles to full takeoff power. The Clipper surged forward and in a few seconds it was riding the step, ready to fly.

At exactly 6 A.M. Bob Ford eased the yoke back. The Clipper broke free and started a long slow climbing turn to the northwest. As they reached 1,000 feet, the sun, rising off their starboard aft quarter, cast long shadows across the land. In a few minutes the coastline was lost to view. As they approached the Great Dividing Range all signs of lakes or rivers disappeared. The Boeing was now a seabird without a place to land. Bob Ford and Johnny Mack stared out of their respective side windows, each silently contemplating the suddenly hostile environment below.

Soon a light rain began falling out of tall cumulus buildups, powered by the heat of the sun as it rose toward its noontime high point. The flat bases of the clouds began to fill in the clear spaces where they could navigate by landmarks. Ford ordered a descent to just below those bases. The ride became a continuous jostling, interspersed with the staccato beat of rain against the fuselage. Taking their heading from the makeshift charts rigged from the old geography books from the Auckland Library, they threaded their way between and beneath the buildups, all the while keeping a hopeful watch for any signs of suitable water landing areas. There were none. Their ears strained for any sign of hesitation in the constant throb of the engines. But they were singing their song of power in complete unison and the pointers on the engine instruments appeared to be painted on their settings. In this way they proceeded into and over the vast 'terra incognita' that was Western Queensland and the Northern Territory of Australia.

After almost eleven hours they could see the horizon ahead opening onto a narrow coastal plain and, beyond that, the welcome sight of water.

"That should be Van Diemen Gulf ahead of us," Rod Brown pointed out. "Darwin should off to the west. Pick up the coast and follow it to the left."

"How does it look for a sheltered landing area?" Ford asked.

"This old map doesn't have much detail, but it looks as though the main Darwin Harbor is fairly well sheltered. Just keep following the coast. It will bear around toward the south and then the harbor should be just there on the west side of that small coastal peninsula area."

Following his navigator's directions, Ford soon picked up the coastline and started a gradual swing toward the west. In a few minutes they were approaching the small port. As they let down, Ford noted that only one large freighter was tied up in the harbor. Following his usually cautious approach, he descended to 500 feet and traversed the length of the area twice. Flags flying on the freighter's mast gave him some indication of the wind direction. Finally, after eleven hours and eleven minutes, NC18602 touched down on the welcome waters of Port Darwin Harbor. There was no suitable floating dock, so they tied up at the first convenient mooring buoy they came to. As they shut down the engines and made the flying boat secure, a small boat from the harbormaster's dock came out to greet them.

Bob Ford stepped out onto the sea wing as the small boat approached. "Ahoy," he called, "Pan American Airways Clipper here. We're out of Auckland bound for New York City. Can we get any 100 octane aviation gas?"

The harbormaster jockeyed the small boat alongside the sea wing. "Aye, Captain, but it's all stored in the warehouse ashore. You'll have to lighter it out here a bit at a time."

"We'll take it. How soon can we get a refueling boat out here?"

"As soon as we get back to shore and load up from the jerry cans," the harbormaster replied. "Can we have some of your crew along to help with the loading?"

"Sure, okay," Ford agreed. "I'll send them along right away."

Ford returned to the flight deck and assigned John Steers, Jocko Parrish, Rod Brown and Johnny Mack to return with the harbormaster to help load the gas. In a few minutes they were pulling up to the dock and they could see that the town was in a state of complete panic.

Soldiers were patrolling the streets, but there was no semblance of order to their movements. People were running everywhere, gathering belongings and piling them on old cars and trucks. Drunken soldiers and sailors were either fighting among themselves or lying passed out on the sidewalks. It was apparent that a lot of beer drinking was going on.

"What the hell is this all about?" Johnny Mack wondered aloud, as they stepped onto the dock and followed the harbormaster to the warehouse where the gasoline was stored.

"Bloody fools, if you ask me!" the harbormaster replied. "Just because the freighter brings in the first supplies of beer any of us has seen for the past six weeks, they all go off their rockers and tank up like cattle at a trough! Some army! It's no wonder everyone's running to get out of town. We've had one air raid already and there's no telling if or when the Japs might take a notion to move onshore here. They sure wouldn't get much of a fight out of these blokes!"

Just then something went flying toward Mack's head. He just had time to make out some sort of shiny object before ducking. The object crashed on the ground and shattered into shards of glass. It was a beer bottle. Mack looked around warily, looking for his attacker. About twenty feet away a very drunk soldier stood, swaying and waving his arms, mouthing incoherent threats at the small group of Pan American crew members. Another soldier, apparently a sergeant, came up behind the bottle thrower and tapped him on the shoulder. As the man turned around, the sergeant let swing with a solid fist and the drunk went down like a log.

"'Ere now, mate," the sergeant exclaimed as he landed the blow, "ya can't go about tossin' missiles at friendly folk like that! Just cool yer arse there for a bloody while!" Then, he tipped his helmet toward Mack and grinned. "Don't mind 'em, mate! They ain't none of 'em 'ad much of a drop the past two weeks and they're just blowin' off a little steam right now! G'day to ya and keep yer guard up!" And with that he turned and marched off down the street.

Despite the sudden attack, Johnny Mack had to grin as he waved his thanks to the sergeant. This was sure a helluva way to run a war! he thought.

When they got to the warehouse they found that the gasoline was stored in hundreds of 5-gallon jerry cans. The harbormaster provided a small lorry and they loaded as many as they could and returned to the dock, where the fuel was transferred to the tanks on a refueling boat. When that load was on the boat, John Steers accompanied it back to the Clipper, while the other three returned to the warehouse to load the lorry again. When the refueling boat reached the Clipper, Steers and Swede Rothe began filling the outboard wing tanks.

All during the refueling operation, darkness fell, and the sky around the harbor was a constant shimmer of lightning as thunderstorms filled the night sky. When a cloudburst would move across the harbor, they had to stop and cover the gas tank inlets to prevent rain water from getting into the tanks. There was nothing they could do then but move down to the cabin and wait for the rain to stop. During one of these waiting periods John Steers looked up with a sudden smile on his face.

"Hell, no point wasting all that good rainwater!" he exclaimed as he jumped up and began to take off his clothes. "This'll be the best shower we've had since leaving Auckland!" And with that he raced up the stairwell, out of the navigator's cargo hatch and stood on top of the wing, letting the welcome and cooling rain wash over his body.

Swede Rothe had looked up, surprised and amused at the naked figure of his crewmate running topside to take advantage of the opportunity.

"Hell," he said to himself aloud, "might as well do it right!" He stopped at the forward lavatory to pick up a small bar of soap before doffing his own clothes and following Steers topside.

"Hey, John!" Rothe called as he emerged from the hatch, "You forgot the soap. Might as well get a real bath while we're at it."

"Hey, good idea!"

Rothe started to lather himself while the downpour continued. The soft rainwater made for a good head of lather as he luxuriated in the unaccustomed pleasure of a cleansing shower. As soon as he had lathered enough he tossed the bar of soap to his partner. The bar fell at Steers' feet. Just as he was about to pick it up the rain stopped. Steers hesitated and looked up.

"Uh-oh!" he called, "Can't rinse off this way. I think I'll pass on the soap." And he laughed as he looked at Swede Rothe, covered and dripping with soap suds.

"Well, goddam! Now what am I supposed to do!" Swede exclaimed, frustrated by the sudden end of the downpour.

"Guess you'll have to dive in and rinse off in the harbor. That storm's pretty well over. No telling how long until another shower comes by." Steers laughingly teased his crewmate.

"What! Jump into that open sewer? There's enough crap and corruption in that bay water to give a guy a permanent case of mildew."

"Well, it's that or sit around and wait. But that ain't getting the gas loaded. Better do something. Skipper wants us out of here by sun-up."

With much swearing and gesturing, Rothe grudgingly went below and out onto the sea wing, where he hesitated; but finally jumped in to rinse off the soap. He climbed out sputtering and swearing. "What a stink. I just hope I don't pick up any creeping crud."

"Don't worry, Swede," Steers tried to assure him, "you're too ornery to catch any bugs. Let's get dried off and get back to work. That gas won't pour itself into the tanks."

With a couple of towels from the stewards' locker, they dried off; Swede Rothe inspecting his limbs and torso for any sign of critters or crud that might have latched onto his skin during his rinse. Once they were dressed, they returned to the chore of hefting the gas hoses from the refueling boat over the wing and filling the outboard wing tanks.

Several trips were needed by all involved to deliver enough fuel to the Clipper to fill the wing tanks. Then they proceeded to fill the two sea wing tanks. By the time they were finished it was 2 A.M.

"Christ! I'm glad that's done," Swede Rothe exclaimed as they passed the refueling hose back to the boat for return to shore. "I don't know about you, but I'm bushed. Let's get some shut-eye. That sunrise is only four hours away."

They crawled into their bunks. Shortly the rest of the crew came back to the ship and also turned in for what little rest they could get. Tomorrow would be even more of a challenge. They would be approaching the war zone and, as confused as the situation was, there was no telling what surprises might be lying in wait.

Radio direction finding on the B-314

Chief Flight Radio Officer Jack Poindexter takes radio direction bearings from the
loop antenna mounted on the roof of the cabin.

CHAPTER IX
A VERY CLOSE CALL

By dawn of December 18th, the thunderstorms had dissipated, but the horizon around Port Darwin was still ringed by towering cumulus clouds. Bob Ford eyed them warily. He knew all too well that they would be the source of renewed thunderstorm weather once the heat of the rising sun began to reinforce the thermal forces that would set them off. He was anxious to take off as soon as possible, but there was one more detail that had to be dealt with before they could leave.

"Our proposed route is going to take us very close to the war action," he explained to the harbormaster, as they prepared to cast off from the buoy. "I don't want any unpleasant surprises. Is there any way we can identify ourselves to Allied forces as we approach Surabaya?"

"We've received some limited procedures from the British and Dutch forces operating up there. I guess it would be okay to pass that along. They have set up some daily challenge and response code words and some identification turns for aircraft approaching the base. I can give you a copy of the pattern. The code words change from day to day and sometimes from hour to hour. About what time do you estimate your arrival at Surabaya?"

Ford did a quick calculation in his head. "If we are off the water by 6 A.M., I figure it should be about 8 or 9 hours to Surabaya. Can't put it much closer, as we don't have any winds aloft data. We're pretty much doing everything on dead reckoning and hoping for the best."

The harbormaster consulted the thick sheaf of papers attached to his clipboard. "It looks as though, for that time slot, they're using a two-word challenge and response procedure. You can do it either by light gun signal, or radio if you want to take a chance on breaking radio silence. They will challenge with the code word B-E-A-M and your response should be H-O-R-N. Got that?"

Ford jotted the two words on the back of an envelope he found in his jacket pocket. "Yeah, roger on that. Thanks. Let's hope it's good for a friendly welcome. And thanks for all your help."

"Oh, and one other thing," the harbormaster added, "I can contact the American Consulate here in Darwin. They should be able to radio the Royal Dutch Air Force base at Surabaya and let them know you are coming."

"That would be a good idea. We can use all the help we can get from here on out. Well... thanks again and I guess we'd better move on out now."

"Glad to have been of service. Frankly, I wouldn't relish being in your shoes. Just be careful and get that big machine back home safe and sound."

The two shook hands. The harbormaster motored back to the dock as Ford stepped back aboard the Boeing. In a few minutes the four engines were roaring again. NC18602 lifted off Port Darwin Harbor just as the sun came up.

With the sun behind them, forward visibility was reasonably good as they stayed below the cumulus bases. Both Ford and First Officer Johnny Mack wanted to keep some sort of landfall in sight as they proceeded into this unknown territory. The Australian coastline soon disappeared into the haze of the tropical morning. Some two and a half hours later they were concentrating their vision forward to seek out the first glimpse of the Indonesian archipelago. But Johnny Mack's mind was taking him back to Hawaii, as he wondered – as he had been wondering ever since the attack on Pearl Harbor – had the Japs invaded Oahu? Had the raid hit the Waikiki area? Questions raced through his mind every day, but there were no answers; only the frustration of not being able to do anything about it except follow the course of action set before them. How long before they would get back – indeed, if they ever did get back?

"Landfall ahead!" Ford's call interrupted Mack's reverie. "Let's check it against that old atlas and see if we can get a positive fix on our position."

"Looks like a pretty long coastline," Mack remarked. "We could be anywhere along that shore. Does the atlas show any identifying landmarks?"

Rod Brown came forward from the navigator's table with the thick atlas in hand. "There really isn't that much to go on, but if we're where I think we ought to be, we should have the island of Timor dead ahead. If you can see the south end of it, there ought to be a small island off there, but if it looks like we have the northern end, there are several even smaller islands. Can you make out anything like that?"

All eyes strained ahead through the maritime haze as the ghostly shoreline came into sharper relief. They scanned the horizon ahead from south to north and back again.

"No breaks that I can see," Mack said. "That shoreline seems to extend as far north and south as we can see. The best I make out, we're somewhere pretty close to the middle of the island."

"In that case," Ford concluded, "let's hold a course straight ahead and cut across to the north side of the chain. Surabaya is on the north side of the island of Java and I'd rather approach it from the over water direction if possible."

As they crossed the shoreline Ford descended to about 4,000 feet. From here, west-northwest bound, he wanted to be low enough to stay below the cloud bases and identify the numerous islands, as they moved along the archipelago, but high enough to make visual contact with the next island before losing sight of the previous one. Soon they had crossed the island of Timor and cut across to the north side of Flores. As soon as they had cleared the north shore, he descended further, maintaining a course parallel to and about a mile offshore of each island as they checked their progress against the atlas. At 4:30 Greenwich time they passed over the island of Bali.

At the Royal Dutch Naval Air Station at Surabaya, the Commandant, Colonel Koenrad, sat at his desk in the squadron operations room. He was reviewing the day's activities. Japanese air raids had been an almost daily occurrence. The damages were relatively light, but the constant harassment had put everyone into a state of tense alertness. His young fighter pilots were a tough lot and spoiling for a fight. They had managed to shoot down a couple of the Japanese bombers, but were still eager for more action.

Koenrad contemplated the sheet of paper on the desk in front of him. It was the day's assignment for patrol flights along the coast.

By now the afternoon group would be patrolling their assigned routes. If they sighted enemy aircraft, they would radio in for additional fighters to be dispatched. But the ground based radio had been troublesome. Sometimes it would not work at all and the patrol pilots would be forced to return to the field to alert the other pilots with visual signals. Today, however, the radio seemed to be working. Koenrad could hear the pilots' conversations as they checked in on their scheduled contacts.

"COBRA, THIS IS A FOR ALBERT. CHECKPOINT ZULU NUL. OVER."

"A FOR ALBERT, THIS IS COBRA, ROGER."

The shorthand phraseology from the fighter called 'A for Albert' indicated that the pilot was over checkpoint Zulu – a small promontory on the north shore about 75 miles east of Surabaya – and that there were no sightings of enemy aircraft. For the time being it was a quiet afternoon.

By this time John Steers was taking his turn in the left seat. As they continued along the Bali coast, he could see numerous thatched-roofed huts jammed together, as they passed several small villages. It all looks so idyllic and peaceful, he mused to himself; hard to believe there's a war going on down there. He looked along the cloud bases to where they merged at the horizon with the higher terrain inland. Then, with the ingrained habit of his pilot training, he shifted his gaze to the instrument panel, monitoring the engine and navigational instruments for any signs of deviation from their established readings. There were none. Once again he scanned the horizon forward and to starboard. Only the towering cumulus and some scattered rain showers ringed their position. He moved his gaze back again toward the shoreline. Then he saw it. Only a speck at first, and then a rapidly growing dark shape.

"Uh-oh!" he muttered aloud.

"What?" Johnny Mack in the right seat caught Steers' exclamation.

"Eleven o'clock, closing fast. Looks like a fighter plane."

"Friend or foe?"

"Can't tell from here, but he's sure coming on like a bat out of hell. What do we do?"

Mack turned in his seat and called to Bob Ford who was conferring with Swede Rothe at the engineer's station. "Skipper, better get up here quick! Looks like we've got company!"

Bob Ford moved quickly forward, motioning Steers to vacate the left seat. "Steady as she goes, Johnny. No fancy maneuvers, Where and how many?"

"Eleven o'clock, maybe three miles and closing fast. Looks like just one."

"Keep on course, no turns, no changes of altitude. Get the light gun ready. If he's friendly he may flash us that recognition code."

At the Surabaya airbase, Colonel Koenrad was just about to leave the operations office when the stillness was shattered by a call on the radio.

"COBRA, THIS IS A FOR ALBERT. SINGLE BOGEY AT ELEVEN, ANGELS FOUR, WESTBOUND. AM PROCEEDING TO INTERCEPT, STAND BY!"

"A FOR ALBERT, COBRA HERE. ROGER BOGEY. WILL YOU NEED BACKUP?"

"CAN'T SAY AS YET. HANG ON..."

A long moment of silence followed as all hands in the operations room waited to hear more.

"COBRA, A FOR ALBERT. SHE'S A BIG ONE, BOYS! SOME KIND OF FLYING BOAT. BETTER COME UP AND HAVE A LOOK-SEE!"

Suddenly the air was filled with the rising wail of the alert sirens. Three Brewster fighters, already 'cocked' for action, darted out of their protective bunkers and lifted off the runway, up and eastward toward whatever it was that was bearing down on them.

Bob Ford gripped the yoke with both hands and concentrated on holding a steady course. He glanced out the wind screen and watched as the Brewster loomed larger in his field of vision. Then he recognized the markings.

"That's a Dutch Air Force plane. I guess we're getting an escort. The American Consul must have got through to the Dutch. We'll follow the recognition pattern as planned."

Meanwhile, at the radio desk, Jack Poindexter had been tuning across the various aircraft bands attempting to pick up the fighters' channel. They could not transmit to them because the crystal-controlled channels of the transmitters were not set for their frequencies; but they might be able to receive instructions and acknowledge with wing movements or turn maneuvers. All at once he picked up a strong signal in mid-transmission.

"...WILL MAINTAIN ESCORT AT HIS SIX O'CLOCK POSITION. REQUEST FURTHER INSTRUCTIONS. OVER"

"A FOR ALBERT, THIS IS COBRA. THREE FRIENDS EN ROUTE. FORM UP AFT OF BOGEY AND MAINTAIN ESCORT. CAN YOU SEE ANY IDENTIFYING MARKS?"

"NOT YET. HOLD ON. WILL ATTEMPT ID. STAND BY."

Bob Ford watched as three more fighters closed in rapidly on the Boeing. They swept past on the port side and then he could not see them. They had taken up positions to the rear of NC18602. Now all four fighters were following the ship.

"Skipper," Poindexter called from the radio desk, "I've picked up their transmissions, but it's a channel we can't transmit on. What do we do?"

"Nothing to do but continue straight and level. We sure as hell don't want to startle them with any sudden change of course. Just keep monitoring and let me know if they broadcast any instructions for us."

"A FOR ALBERT, THIS IS B FOR BRAVO. THAT'S A MIGHTY FINE TARGET WE HAVE THERE. WHY TAKE A CHANCE. I THINK WE SHOULD BLAST IT NOW. SHALL I LET HIM HAVE IT?"

"B FOR BRAVO, HOLD ON CHAP. WE NEED GROUND OKAY. THEY WANT AN ID BEFORE WE SHOOT. BESIDES, HE SEEMS TO BE RATHER DOCILE AT THE MOMENT. DON'T SEE ANY ARMAMENTS AND HE HASN'T MADE ANY EVASIVE MANEUVERS. HOLD YOUR BEAD ON HIM. I'M GOING IN OVER HIS TOPSIDE TO SEE IF THERE IS ANY ID ON HIM."

"Captain," Poindexter called to Ford, "they're closing in to get an identification on us. Sounds like they're really itchy to shoot us down!"

"Damn!" Ford muttered under his breath, "Why did we take our ID marks off at Auckland? We could sure use those markings now!"

A for Albert slowly closed the distance between them and climbed to an altitude just a few feet above the Boeing's triple tail. As he moved forward he spotted the remains of the American flag that had not been removed from the top of the wing.

"COBRA, A FOR ALBERT HERE. THERE APPEARS TO BE PART OF AN AMERICAN FLAG PAINTED ON THE TOP

SURFACE OF THE WING. NO OTHER IDENTIFYING MARKS VISIBLE. ADVISE PLEASE."

Colonel Koenrad stood behind the radio desk and pondered what he had just heard. Anyone could paint flags on aircraft. Any deception was possible. On the other hand, the bogey had not made any attempt to evade the intercept and was maintaining a straight and level course. Could he take a chance on it being friendly? His decision had to be made now.

"A FOR ALBERT, THIS IS COBRA." Koenrad took the microphone from the radio operator and spoke to the fighter himself. "MAINTAIN SURVEILLANCE IN FORMATION AT HIS SIX O'CLOCK POSITION. KEEP GUNS READY. LET HIM PROCEED AND WE'LL SEE WHAT HE DOES. IF HE SO MUCH AS WAGGLES A WING THE WRONG WAY, TAKE HIM OUT!"

"COBRA, A FOR ALBERT, ROGER. BOYS, YOU ALL HEARD THAT. FORM UP AFT AND KEEP YOUR SAFETIES OFF. WE GO WHERE HE GOES."

In this way, like a great whale followed by pilot fish, the Boeing continued on its straight-in course toward the bay at Surabaya. As they approached one of the recognition checkpoints, Ford, gently and slowly, eased around in a procedure turn over the point, as they had been instructed to do by the Aussies.

"COBRA, A FOR ALBERT. BOGEY APPEARS TO BE MAKING VALID IDENTIFICATION TURN OVER POINT X-RAY."

"A FOR ALBERT, COBRA. ROGER ON THAT. CONTINUE ESCORT."

Bob Ford glanced back along his port side as he completed the turn. He could just barely make out two of the fighter planes as they followed him in the turn. "Well," he remarked, "they seem to have accepted that maneuver. Now let's see if they'll let us approach and land. Swede, set us up for a standard rate of descent, slow to approach speed and one-quarter flaps."

"Aye, Captain." Swede responded. "And all fuel pumps on, fuel on mains, mixtures full rich, ready for approach and landing."

They were now approaching the sheltered strait separating Surabaya and the island of Madura. Ford concentrated his view ahead, trying to discover a safe landing area. The harbor at Surabaya was crowded with all kinds of ships. There did not appear to be a really safe seaplane landing area. The area just outside the harbor breakwater appeared to be the most suitable.

"Johnny, set us up for an approach parallel to that breakwater, just outside the entrance to the harbor. We'll put down as close to the entrance as possible and then taxi in."

"Okay, Skipper."

The Boeing eased around in a gentle turn onto the final approach. The Brewster fighters followed as if they were connected to the flying boat by a leash. Easing down to about fifty feet above the water, Ford made a long, slow final approach. The touchdown was feather-light. Just as Ford pulled the throttles to idle and hauled back on the yoke to slow their forward speed, the Brewsters roared past overhead.

"COBRA, A FOR ALBERT. BOGEY HAS TOUCHED DOWN JUST OUTSIDE THE ENTRANCE TO THE INNER HARBOR. SHALL WE CONTINUE TO FOLLOW? OVER."

"A FOR ALBERT, ROGER. WE HAVE ALERTED THE HARBORMASTER. THEY ARE SENDING A PATROL BOAT TO INTERCEPT. YOU MAY RESUME YOUR SCHEDULED COASTAL PATROL. AND GOOD WORK CHAPS. WE'LL TAKE IT FROM HERE."

"ROGER, COBRA. OKAY BOYS, RESUME ORIGINAL PATROL PATTERNS. A FOR ALBERT OUT."

As the fighters broke off the intercept and made a wide circling climb to resume their patrol duties, Ford swung the Boeing around and started taxiing toward the breakwater entrance. As he moved slowly toward the inner harbor he saw the patrol boat coming toward them. A figure standing in the bow was waving at them, signaling for the ship to follow them into the harbor.

"We seem to have a surface escort," Johnny Mack remarked, pointing at the distant boat. "Shall we follow him in?"

"Just proceed slowly," Ford replied, "They might still be a little trigger-happy. We'll keep our distance until we see where they're leading us."

With the vision of the Dutch fighter planes still vivid in his mind, Bob Ford forced himself to concentrate on the priority of the moment: get this flying boat safely tied up at a buoy or dock and find out what the hell happened to that prior notification that the Aussies were supposed to send to the Dutch. With half a world further to go before reaching home, he did not want any more foul-ups that would threaten the safety of the plane or crew. It was tough enough doing this with no advance planning, let alone having to worry about challenges from friendly forces as well as enemy threats.

With just enough throttle to maintain headway across the channel to the harbor entrance, Ford proceeded to follow the boat. Upon clearing the harbor entrance, the small boat headed directly toward a large buoy just off-shore from a small dock. The figure in the bow continued to wave the Clipper toward the buoy.

"Looks as though they want us to tie up there," Mack said, pointing at the buoy.

"Okay, Steers, Brown, into the bow." Ford called, "They're putting us on a buoy."

John Steers and Rod Brown left their positions and crawled through the forward hatch into the bow compartment. With the bow hatch removed, they soon had the buoy lines secured to the snubbing posts and Ford shut down all engines. NC18602 swung lazily into the wind as the patrol boat pulled alongside the port sea wing.

"Everyone stay on board," Ford ordered, "until we can sort out our status. That fighter escort acted as if they didn't know about us. I'll try to find out what happened to that notification that was supposed to have been sent."

He went below and stepped out on the port sea wing as the boat pulled alongside.

"Ahoy! Captain," the officer in the boat called out. "Please come aboard. You will have to report to our headquarters. We must escort you ashore."

"Okay," Ford replied, "but I must leave my crew on board for now. It will take some time for them to secure our craft."

"That will be satisfactory, Captain. By the way, what kind of aircraft is this? And where did you come from? We had no information about you."

"This is a Pan American B314 Clipper. We were headed into Auckland when we learned about the Japanese attack on Pearl Harbor. They gave us orders to divert westbound and try to get back to the United States the long way round to avoid getting caught by the Japanese."

"That is very interesting. But you will have to see our commanding officer before we can clarify your status. Strictly for security reasons, you understand."

Ford nodded his assent as he boarded the boat and they proceeded to the dock. Once on shore, they walked across the road to the administration building. Colonel Koenrad was coming down the steps as they approached.

"Captain, good afternoon." Koenrad extended his hand. "I'm Colonel Koenrad. I trust you can enlighten me as to the reason for your unannounced arrival?"

Ford shook the extended hand and proceeded to explain the situation, taking care to mention that they had expected the Australians to relay information about their arrival and that, apparently, there had been some sort of breakdown in communications.

Koenrad considered this explanation. "Well, Captain, it is very possible that, considering the confused situation, red tape and all that, that the message about your arrival has been delayed somewhere. I must say, however, that you and your crew are very lucky fellows. Our fighter boys have been itching for a fight ever since the Japanese attack. Normally our attack orders are issued on the ground-air radio. We have been having severe supply problems and the condition of our communications equipment is somewhat precarious. You were very fortunate that the radio was working today, because most of the time it is not. Without direct orders from me it is highly likely that our fighters would have shot you down just as a precaution. You understand, of course, that we can not be too careful. We have had several air raids in the past few weeks and the situation is very tense."

"That's understandable," Ford said with a wry smile

"And of course," Koenrad added, "we were very concerned when you landed outside the breakwater in the open channel. You see, that area is heavily mined as a protection against enemy surface ships approaching the harbor. That is why our patrol boat kept its distance while waving you in. It seems you and your crew were doubly lucky."

Ford shook his head at this description of the second and unknown threat to the flight. "So it seems. I hope we don't have that kind of a gauntlet to run elsewhere in our journey. However," and here he changed the subject, "I hope we can arrange to have advance notification of our proposed route forwarded with some assurance that it will be delivered. Is there any way we can arrange for confirmed notifications? I can give you a list of our proposed stopover points."

Koenrad took note of Ford's list of proposed stops and promised to do his best to have the confirmed messages sent ahead.

"Also, Colonel," Ford asked, "we will need to refuel with 100 octane aviation fuel. We have US dollars to pay for it."

Koenrad frowned. "I'm sorry Captain, but our supply of 100 octane is very limited. We must give priority to our fighter aircraft. However, we can off regular 90 octane, if you can use that."

Ford considered this for a moment. He knew that anything less than 100 octane could cause mis-firing and cylinder damage if the high compression GR2600 engines were to run on the lower octane fuel for any extended time. But they had just about used up their load of 100 octane on the flight from Darwin. There appeared to be no choice but to take the 90 octane and hope for the best.

"Very well. I'll check with my flight engineer. We may be able to adjust our fuel mixtures to compensate for the lower octane. Meanwhile, are there any overnight accommodations we can use?"

"Our barracks are totally occupied. There is only one hotel in town – the Orange – but it is booked full also. Three of your American Naval ships are in port and most of the seamen are on shore leave. Some expect to depart tomorrow, but for this evening there seems to be no available accommodations."

"In that case we'll just spend the night on board the aircraft. Can I bring my crew ashore for dinner? And then we'll return to the ship for the night."

"Yes, that will be satisfactory," Koenrad agreed. "But if you will continue to Ceylon and India, we must insist that you and your crew be given inoculations for typhus, dysentery, and cholera. The sanitary conditions in some of the places you will be going to are considered very risky at this time."

Ford frowned and shrugged. "Well, if we must... I'll have the crew available when you can arrange it."

They shook hands again and Ford returned to the Clipper. The rest of the crew boarded the boat and went ashore. In the Dutch pilots' officers' mess they talked with the young fighter pilots who, earlier, had almost shot them down. They all agreed that the Clipper crew had been very, very lucky.

Following dinner, Ford and his crew returned to the Clipper. On the verge of exhaustion, each of them selected a bunk and promptly dozed off for a long-delayed good night's sleep. Refueling the Boeing would have to wait until morning.

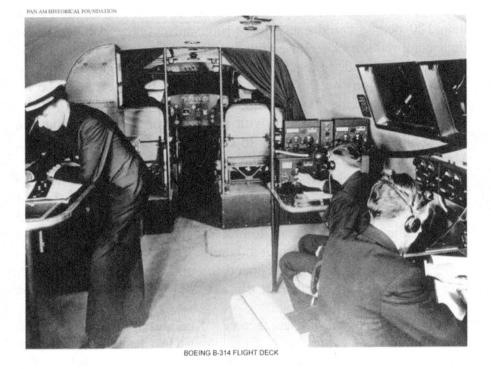

BOEING B-314 FLIGHT DECK

Crew members at their stations on the flight deck.
From L to R: Navigator, Pilot and Co-Pilot, Radio Officer, Engineering Officer

CHAPTER X
EDGE OF THE WAR ZONE

On the morning of December 19th, John Steers heard the sound first. He had slept in one of the main cabin bunks near the sea wing entry hatch. The banging sound seemed far off at first, as if it were part of some dream. But, as it continued to intrude on his senses, he awoke to realize that someone was banging on the hatch from the outside.

"Okay! Okay!" he finally called aloud. "Just a minute!"

When he opened the hatch he saw the harbormaster from the evening before standing on the sea wing smiling at him.

"Good morning, sir!" the harbormaster greeted him. "May we speak to your captain? We need to arrange for your refueling. Also we can take you ashore for breakfast if you wish."

"Yeah, okay," Steers replied, still groggy from too little sleep. "Just a minute and I'll get him for you."

He made his way to the forward crew compartment where Bob Ford had bunked down. By now the rest of the crew were also stirring awake.

"What is it, Johnny?" Ford asked, as he crawled out of the bunk.

"The Dutch harbormaster is alongside. Wants to see about refueling. And he says we can come ashore for breakfast."

"Okay, I'll talk to him. Might as well do that. The refueling could take some time."

Ford came to the open hatch where the harbormaster was waiting. "Good morning, sir. I understand you are ready to refuel us?"

"Yes, Captain. My crew can bring the petrol out as soon as you give the word."

"Let me talk to my flight engineer first. Your Colonel Koenrad said we could get only 90 octane auto gas. We may have to make some fuel management adjustments to compensate for the lower octane. Shouldn't take too long. Meanwhile, can you take the rest of my crew ashore?"

"Yes, that will be fine. We'll take them ashore, then return with the petrol."

All the crew members, except Ford, Swede Rothe, and Jocko Parrish, boarded the patrol boat and went ashore. As soon as they were clear, Ford turned to Rothe.

"Swede," he explained, "they can only give us 90 octane auto gas. What's the status of our remaining 100 octane?"

"The lower sea wing tanks are down to one third and the outboard mains are just about dry. I suggest we transfer all the remaining 100 octane to the inboard mains where we can reserve it for takeoff and landing. Load the 90 octane into the other tanks and try to use it only for en route cruising. That way, if we run into any power problems like pre-detonation or backfiring it won't be during critical takeoff or landing operations."

"Okay, let's do it."

The trio returned to the flight deck. Rothe powered up the auxiliary power generator and switched on the fuel transfer pumps. Soon, the remaining 100 octane was transferred from the sea wing tanks and outboard tanks to the main inboards. Rothe studied the gauges on the main tanks.

"It's not as much as I'd like to see," he advised Ford, "but it should be enough for takeoff and climb to altitude. I just hope we won't have to fly on that 90 octane stuff for too long. Even leaned out to optimum, we're likely to get some backfiring and high cylinder temps that could raise hell with the pistons."

"I agree, Swede, but we don't have much choice. It's either take the 90 octane or be stranded here for who knows how long before they'd agree to give us the 100 octane. And this war isn't getting any better. The sooner we can get this ship out of the war zone, the better I'll feel about our situation."

"Yeah, I guess you're right. We'll just have to play it by ear. My guess is that we're going to need some of those spare engine parts we've got on board before we get back to Company territory."

A refueling boat with the load of 90 octane gas was dispatched to the Clipper. As soon as the sea wing and outboard wing tanks had been filled, Ford and his two flight engineers secured the ship and went ashore to join the other crew members at the officers' mess for breakfast. As they were finishing their meal, Colonel Koenrad approached their table.

"Good morning, gentlemen." He greeted them cordially. "I trust you slept well?"

"As well as can be expected, under the circumstances." Ford replied.

"I can now inform you that accommodations will be available at the Orange Hotel later this afternoon. One of your American ships is leaving then, and that will make rooms available. Also, it will be necessary for you to report to our infirmary to get your inoculations before you leave. Our doctors are quite busy today, but we have arranged for you to see them first thing tomorrow."

"That's fine, Colonel," Ford said. "Meanwhile I'd like to arrange for a couple of my crew members to return to the ship in the evening to stand security watch."

"No problem, Captain. Just have them check in at the harbormaster's office and they can arrange ferry service to your ship."

Ford assigned Jim Henricksen and Rod Brown to take the second evening's security watch aboard the Clipper. The rest of the crew, with nothing but time on their hands, strolled around the town. It took a while to get used to the traffic driving on the left.

"Hey, look there," John Steers exclaimed, "I do believe that's a beer joint!" He pointed in the direction of a rather nondescript building which appeared very crowded and from which they could hear the familiar beat of someone banging out a boogie-woogie tune on a piano.

"Boy, I could sure use a cool brew right about now," Swede Rothe added. "Let's give it a try."

As they entered the beer parlor they could see it was crowded with American sailors. One of them was at the piano, pounding out the boogie beat they had heard from the street. The dark interior of the building provided some relief from the heat of the mid-day sun outside. The piano player's buddies were keeping his glass filled for him as he performed. Everyone else was gulping down the brew as if they were making up for lost time from having been at sea too long. It was a raucous, but friendly crowd that made way for the Pan American crew as they edged their way in and bellied up to the bar. Soon all the crew members were hoisting froth-topped mugs. By 4

P.M. the heat had slackened off a little and the crew finally made their way to the Orange Hotel. What with the long hot day, waiting for rooms, and the unexpected beer drinking, they were all soon catching up on a good night's sleep.

John Steers awoke to the sound of early morning traffic outside the open window of his hotel room. Still bleary from the effects of all the beer drinking the evening before, he pushed aside the carefully tucked-in mosquito netting and sat up on the edge of the bed. The morning air was very cool in contrast with the heat of the day before. He shivered slightly and rubbed his eyes.

Guess I better hit the shower, he thought; might help get rid of the fuzziness. He stood and walked to the open window and stared down for a moment. The three-wheel taxis were sputtering up and down the street. Pretty Javanese women, carrying all sorts of loads on their heads, made their way through the market crowds in stately posture. A few soldiers in a jeep sat at the intersection smoking cigarettes. Except for the soldiers, it was hard to tell that a war was going on. Steers shivered again in the cool morning air, then turned and sought out the shower stall. He had no sooner started lathering up when the air raid sirens sounded.

"Oh, shit!" he muttered to himself, "Now what?"

Hurriedly he rinsed off, wrapped a bath towel around his waist and ran to the window to see what was happening. The scene was totally changed from a few minutes earlier. People were scurrying in all directions. The soldiers in the jeep were roaring off toward the harbor. All was pandemonium. But there was no sign of enemy aircraft as far as Steers could see. The sky was bright and quiet. Off in the distance there was a low hum that could have been aircraft, but it was too far away to identify as either friend or foe. Steers decided that he had time to get dressed and try to find his fellow crew members to see if they knew what was happening.

By the time he got to the lobby the other crew members were gathering around Bob Ford, trying to decide what to do. The Clipper was a sitting duck, moored in the harbor, and they had to move fast if they were to get it airborne and out of whatever danger was implicit in the air raid alarm.

"I say we make a run for the dock, get a launch, get the hell out to the ship, and high-tail it out of here." Jocko Parrish suggested.

"How do the rest of you feel about that?" Ford polled the crew.

"Yeah!"

"Hell, we could die trying, but I can't see sitting here doing nothing."

"Let's go, then, but everyone keep your head up. Just stay together and follow me." Ford ordered.

Just as they reached the street, the all-clear sounded.

"Now, what the hell?" Swede Rothe blurted.

"Must have been a false alarm. Maybe today's the day they test the system."

"No," Ford added, "I don't think they'd do that during wartime. Too much of a chance they'd mistake a real raid for a drill some time. But I think we need to get down there anyway, just to check things out."

As they approached the harbor they could see what had caused the alarm. Taxiing in from the breakwater were several Consolidated PBY flying boats. They all had U.S. Navy markings. Colonel Koenrad stood at the edge of the dock waiting to greet the first PBY crew as they came ashore. Ford approached and stood next to the Colonel.

"Who are they?" Ford asked.

"I don't know, Captain," Koenrad replied, "but the situation looks very similar to your arrival."

Soon the PBY crews came ashore. Colonel Koenrad greeted each of them and soon the reason for their arrival became clear. They were the last surviving PBY patrol squadron to have escaped from Cavite in the Philippines.

Bob Ford greeted the pilot of the last PBY to land. "Glad to see you made it okay," he said as he shook the Navy pilot's hand, "We're sort of on the run ourselves."

"Yeah, I spotted that big flying boat when we came in. Sure hope you have better luck getting out of here than we had getting out of Cavite."

"Oh, how's that?"

"We just made it out of there by the skin of our teeth. There was one other PBY in our squadron. They got him just as he was lifting off the water. Poor bastards never had a chance."

"Sorry to hear that," Ford said quietly. "Now what do you do?"

"Wait for orders from CINCPAC I guess. Most likely be assigned patrol duties out of here in the meantime. Can't really say for sure. This is one helluva screwed-up war as far as communications is concerned!"

"You've got that right!" Ford acknowledged. "We had a royal welcome when we came in the other day. It was pucker time for sure there, for a while. I'm just hoping we can clear up that situation for the rest of our flight."

"Well, lots of luck, Captain. Just keep your guard up the rest of the way and you should be okay. By the way, where are you headed anyway?"

Ford hesitated for a moment. He was remembering the Plan A directive about secrecy. But this was a Navy pilot he was talking to. What harm could it do? "We're supposed to get back to the States as best we can. Right now we're taking the long way round by heading west. It's sort of a crap shoot at this point because we've never flown a Pan Am Clipper in these parts before. You could say we're really 'winging' this one." There, he'd explained it without really giving out any specific information. That should do.

"Well, I wish I was coming with you. I have a hunch we'll be driving these PBYs around here for quite a while. See you when the war's over!" and he extended his hand. Ford shook it and the two pilots nodded silently toward each other. Then the Navy pilot turned to join his fellow crew members as they went with Colonel Koenrad to the debriefing session in the administration building.

As Colonel Koenrad had promised, the crew was called to the base infirmary to receive shots for typhus, dysentery, and cholera. The Dutch doctor had a peculiar procedure for administering the shots. Instead of the usual place – in the upper arm – he put them in just above the nipple of the left breast. Jack Poindexter and Barney Sawicki turned so pale that the doctor thought they were going to faint. He quickly sat them down and shoved their heads between their legs. Eugene Leach passed out in a dead faint and had to be revived with smelling salts. Bob Ford got a severe case of the chills and shivered all night, even with his raincoat wrapped around him.

Swede Rothe, stoic as ever, managed a wry grin as the doctor inserted the needle. "Hey, that must be pretty strong stuff, doc!" What do you have in there, Mickey Finns?"

"No, sir," the doctor replied, "but it is a fairly new and potent safeguard against typhus, dysentery, and cholera. Considering where you intend to go, it is just as well we give you a little discomfort now in exchange for some protection later. All our reports indicate that

108

those diseases are raging almost out of control further up into the sub-continent. The war seems to have caused a considerable breakdown in sanitary conditions."

"Well," Swede concluded, "I guess you're the doc and I won't argue with that. Just so those boys are up and ready to fly by morning."

"Oh, yes." the doctor assured him, "These symptoms are very temporary. I assure you they'll all be fine by tomorrow."

With the shots taken care of and the 90 octane gasoline loaded on board the Clipper, all but two of the crew returned to the Orange Hotel. Rod Brown and Jocko Parrish returned to the Clipper to stand security watch for the night. It was clear that the false air raid alarm, caused by the arrival of the U.S. Navy PBYs, had only increased the tension in the air. Everyone was speculating on the imminence of the next real air raid. The trouble was there was nothing anyone could do about it, which only added to the sense of frustration. Ford went to bed early, wrapped in his raincoat, trying to overcome the chills that shook his wiry frame. The rest of the crew was not disposed to much in the way of an evening's entertainment at the local beer parlor again. All of them bedded down early and sought to revive their energies by getting a good night's sleep. Tomorrow's flight was going to be one of the longest legs thus far. As best as they could figure out from their makeshift charts, the journey to Trincomalee on the island of Ceylon[7] would take the better part of twenty hours. And they had the unknown quantity of trying to operate on auto gas with engines designed for 100 octane. It was going to be an interesting flight.

---

[7] Present day Sri Lanka

MARINE AIR TERMINAL AT LAGUARDIA AIRPORT 1940s
DESIGNED BY DELANO & ALDRICH, AS WAS PAA'S DINNER KEY TERMINAL

The Marine Air Terminal as it looked when NC18602 arrived in New York on
January 6, 1942.

CHAPTER XI
ACROSS AN UNKNOWN SEA

"Swede," Bob Ford huddled with his First Engineer, "we need to conserve as much of our remaining 100 octane as possible. As soon as we have a safe altitude – say a couple of thousand feet – we'll level out and switch to the 90 octane tanks."

"Okay," Rothe replied, "but it's strictly a crap-shoot as to what might happen when we try to lean out to cruise power. Those cylinder head temps could go through the roof and we could blow a jug."

"I'm aware of that. It's not like we have any kind of choice at this point. If we can maintain enough power without pushing redline on the cylinders, well, that's all we'll need to do until we can get to Trincomalee. After that, we'll just have to see."

Swede nodded in agreement. He resumed his place at the engineer's desk and concentrated his vision and thoughts on the big panel in front of him. Ford climbed into the left seat and gave a thumbs-up sign to Johnny Mack. It was time to go.

They left Surabaya in late afternoon. They would have to fly through the night to arrive in Trincomalee in daylight. A night flight had one other advantage: flying blacked-out would provide less chance for detection by Japanese patrol planes; which probably would not fly at night anyway.

As soon as they reached 2,000 feet, Ford leveled off and gave the order to switch to the 90 octane tanks. Swede Rothe reached for the large circular fuel valve handles. "Fuel pumps on, cross-feed on," he called out instinctively as he slowly moved the valves from top center mains to the sea wing tanks; all the time concentrating his vision on the fuel flow and cylinder head temperature gauges. The fuel gauges fluctuated momentarily, then stabilized. They were now flying on auto gas; a condition never contemplated by the engineers at Boeing or at the Wright engine factory.

"How's it look, Swede?" Ford asked.

"So far, so good. Cylinder head temps seem to be holding. But we're flying full rich. We're going to have to lean it out for best fuel range."

"Okay, just watch those gauges. Let's do it a little bit at a time."

Very slowly, Rothe pulled back the mixture controls. As the levers came back, each increment changed the ratio of gas to air so that the amount of air increased while the amount of fuel burning in the cylinders decreased. "Manifold pressure coming up," he reported, "Looks good so far."

"Okay, come on back more."

Another increment; another increase in manifold pressure. Then: "Skipper, the cylinder head temps are starting up."

"Roger. Just keep an eye on them."

Rothe continued leaning out the fuel flow. Manifold pressure increased, then slowed and began to decrease. They had reached optimum mixture. He readjusted the mixture to maintain the peak manifold pressure. But the cylinder head temperatures kept rising. "Head temps five degrees below redline," he called out.

"What's the maximum under redline we can sustain?"

"Don't know, Skipper. We've never flown it this way before. If we were redlining with 100 octane we'd have some chart parameters to go by but this auto stuff is..."

BANG! The sudden sound filled the cabin and the Clipper shook as though it were in the grip of a gigantic storm.

BANG! Again.

"Backfiring on Numbers Two and Three!" Johnny Mack called out. "Those cowlings are shaking like Jell-o!"

"Back off the mixture, Swede!" Ford shouted.

Rothe quickly moved the mixture controls toward the rich side of their range. Just as quickly the banging stopped. But the cylinder head temperatures remained just under redline.

"Okay, let's regroup and try again. We want a setting just under where the backfiring starts. Can you get a feel for that, Swede?"

"Aye, Skipper. But those head temps aren't coming down any."

"Never mind the head temps. As long as we can find a mixture that won't backfire, we'll run with that. Try it again."

Once again the mixture controls came back. Once again the manifold pressures increased and the cylinder head temperatures rested within a degree of the forbidden redline. Then: BANG! BANG! The Clipper shook as though it were a rag doll in the hands of a very active child. Quickly, but with more control this time, Rothe eased the mixture controls back to just under the mark where the backfiring would start. "That's about the best we can do," he called out. "We can stay below the backfire point, but I can't guarantee the head temps. They're just about out of normal range for long-range cruise."

"As long as we can control the backfiring and they're running smoothly otherwise, let's go with it. We'll just have to stay at this altitude Just keep your eyes on those gauges."

Using their atlas and makeshift charts, Rod Brown plotted a dog-leg course out of Surabaya, west to the Sunda Strait, then southwest through the strait and then northwest along the southwest coast of Sumatra. As the sun set they threaded their way along the Sumatra coast, staying in the long channel between the main island and the chain of small islands paralleling the coastline. Night fell as they approached the far northwestern end of Sumatra.

"There goes our last positive landfall. Rod, do you have the DR heading to Trincomalee?" Ford asked, turning toward his Second Officer who was bent over the navigator's table in deep concentration.

"Yes sir, coming up right away." Brown answered. Then he jotted down the numbers on a small square of paper and handed it to Ford.

"275 degrees," Ford noted. "Any allowance for magnetic variation on that?"

"No, sir," Brown explained, "the best I can make out from the Bowdich's manual, this far around the globe we can just about draw a straight line that would run through the North Pole and the Magnetic Pole without much variation. Even if we miss Ceylon Island, we'd have a landfall on the Indian coastline that could lead us to Ceylon."

"Try to get some star sights too. I'd just as soon not have to do too much backtracking."

They continued into the night across, what was to them, an unknown sea. Soon, unseen by the crew, the southern islands of the

Nicobar chain passed abeam their starboard wing. Brown was able to get two star sightings before clouds began to close in overhead. With the engines leaned out as far as the 90 octane gas would allow without backfiring and the cylinder head temperatures hovering just under the redline, they could not risk climbing higher to get above the clouds.

Soon it began to rain; intermittently at first, then continuously, as the hours dragged by. Crew members observed their duty rotation schedules with barely a word of conversation. The mechanics and off duty crew members on the lower deck slept fitfully amid the clutter and close confines created by all the spare parts. The night became an endurance contest between the crew and the machine. The pilots were now flying totally on instruments as the lowering rain clouds obscured any physical view of the ocean or sky. It was as though they were all in a sort of endless black limbo; jostled by the intermittent turbulence, listening to the staccato sound of rain against the fuselage and the constant drone of the engines. The world outside had ceased to exist. They were alone in the universe, and there was no end in sight to their journey.

Dawn came slowly. As the darkness paled they were still enveloped in a continuous grey cocoon of clouds and rain. They had now been airborne for the better part of 19 hours. According to the dead reckoning estimate that Rod Brown had posted on their makeshift chart, they should soon make landfall off the coast of Ceylon. But, shrouded as they were by the gloomy amorphous grayness around them, there was no way to detect the presence of land.

"I guess we're going to have to get underneath this stuff to get any kind of visual landfall," Ford remarked. "We'd better start down. I don't much relish the idea of missing the island and having to backtrack while our fuel reserve gets used up."

Swede Rothe eased back on the throttles and increased the mixture toward full rich as they began a slow descent, feeling their way toward the bottom of the cloud deck. Soon they were breaking in and out of ragged cloud formations. The ocean below appeared grey and foam-flecked. Intermittent rain created sudden bursts of sound against the hull as they went lower still.

"That's far enough, Swede." Ford called out, s they reached a mere 300 feet above the waves. "Level off here. It looks like visibility is improving up ahead."

114

Now clear of the cloud bases, they could see the extent of the storm they had been flying through. All around them to the north, east, and south, the grey roiling scud protruded from higher layers extending out of sight above them. Ahead, to the west, they could see brighter areas interspersed with rain shafts. Visibility beneath the scud appeared to be good – about 20 to 30 miles, Ford estimated. Good, he thought, if we're anywhere near on course, we should make the Ceylon landfall without any problem.

In the right seat, Johnny Mack stretched and yawned. It had been a long, tiring night. Soon they would land and he could look forward to a decent breakfast and a few hours rest. He rubbed his eyes to clear his vision, stretched again and scanned the brightening horizon for signs of a landfall. The sea was silvery grey against the early morning light. Then he saw it: in the water dead ahead, a small dark spot at first and then it kept getting larger. Hmm, he mused to himself, that can't be land. It's too small. Whales, maybe? Or a small boat, he questioned himself as he watched the spot grow.

"Hey, Skipper," Mack remarked idly, "what do you suppose that is, there, dead ahead. A whale, maybe?"

Bob Ford glanced ahead to where Mack was pointing. The dark object had grown longer. A foamy wave surged up ahead of it. All at once it's identity became clear.

"Submarine!" Ford shouted. "But I can't see any ID marks."

"Is it Japanese?"

"Hell, we'll soon find out! At this range we can't turn sharp enough. We're going to fly right over it!"

As the long, thin hull emerged from the water, the conning tower became visible. Painted on the side, clearly visible, was the Rising Sun flag of the Imperial Japanese Navy. In just seconds they could see human figures running forward toward a deck gun.

"Hey, they're aiming that thing at us!" Mack shouted.

"Swede!" Ford yelled to the engineer. "Full rich, full power, max climb! Let's get the hell out of here!"

As the engines turned up to full power, Ford hauled back on the yoke and sought maximum climb rate from the Clipper. If they could get above the cloud base again, the cloud cover might shield them from the gun crew. As the Clipper roared past the submarine, Mack could see the sub crew swing the deck gun around. Come on, baby, he implored the Boeing, come on! Come on! Climb, you sweetheart, climb!

Holding his best rate-of-climb speed, Ford aimed for the nearest low scud. Though it seemed like an eternity, in a few seconds they were penetrating the bottom of the clouds. Soon they were once again surrounded by the wet, grey, impenetrable blanket. Just as they went back on instruments, a bright flash illuminated the clouds below them. The sub had fired the deck gun. They all tensed for the expected impact. Nothing happened. They were still climbing.

"Phew!" Ford exhaled. "That was downright unfriendly. Swede, reset power for level cruise. I think we're okay now."

"Right," Rothe acknowledged, as he pulled the throttles back. He left the mixtures at full rich. This was no time to risk backfiring and possible loss of power that would force them below the clouds.

In about ten minutes Ford felt safe to descend below the cloud bases again. By now, he thought, we should be out of range of that deck gun. "I think we can let down again, Swede. We should be far enough past that sub to be out of range of their guns. And I still don't want to miss that island. Our reserves are low enough as it is without having to muck about trying to get back on course if we miss it."

"God!" Johnny Mack exclaimed. "If only we'd had a torpedo, or a bomb, we could have really blown that sucker out of the water."

"Yeah, well, I guess they were as surprised as we were," Ford added. "But the best we can do now is to report it to the British command at Trincomalee. Maybe they can send out patrols to this area. If we give them a good enough fix on it they should be able to spot it. Hey, Rod," he added, turning to Rod Brown at the navigator's table, "how close a fix can we get on that intercept?"

Brown consulted his makeshift navigation chart. They had been flying a fairly straight compass course ever since the western end of Sumatra the evening before. Banking on the winds aloft averaging out, considering the length of their flight thus far, he figured an intercept location that he hoped would fall well within the search capabilities of the British patrol squadrons.

"Here, Skipper," he brought his worksheet to Ford. "This fix ought to do it."

Ford glanced at the chart and the notation. "8 degrees, 40 minutes north, 83 degrees, 30 minutes east." Ford observed the coordinates. "That puts them pretty close in to their coastal shipping lanes. I'll bet the British High Command will be glad to get this information."

"Hey, land ho!" Johnny Mack exclaimed.

Ahead, in the narrow corridor between the sea and the lower cloud level, there appeared a brighter horizon with a dark, long shoreline just above it. All eyes strained forward, hoping to catch a glimpse of some prominent terrain or landmark that they could identify from the atlas.

"Drop down to 500 feet," Ford ordered. "Let's take that shoreline head on. We need to figure which way to turn when we cross over the beach."

"I'm pretty sure we should head north along that coast, Bob," Brown advised. "Even if we're past Trincomalee, we'd find out real soon by running up against the Indian coast right quick."

"Okay. We'll bear right and start looking for that harbor."

Brown's navigation turned out to be reasonably close. Within about 45 minutes after the encounter with the submarine, they spotted the harbor at Trincomalee. Fifteen minutes later the Clipper was cutting its bright foam-flecked landing swath along the seaplane channel. A British tender came out from the dock and helped them secure the Clipper to a seaplane buoy. This time, it seemed, word of their progress had, indeed, been relayed along the line. The greeting from the tender pilot was friendly and familiar.

"Good morning, mates," the tender pilot called out. "We've been expecting you. It's Captain Ford, is it not?"

"Yes," Ford answered as he came out the main cabin hatch and stood on the sea wing. "I guess our Dutch friends got word to you about us."

"Got the word through our diplomatic code office. Not much detail, but they said you'd be a big one. And, blimey, they were right! What sort of bird is this anyway?" The British ground staff were familiar with the Short 'Empire' S-23 flying boats, the same size as the Sikorsky S-42, but they had seen nothing like the big Boeing.

Ford proceeded to explain about NC18602 and the circumstances of their journey. When he had finished, the rest of the crew came out and, except for Johnny Mack and Jocko Parrish, they boarded the tender for the ride to shore. Mack and Parrish stayed aboard the Clipper as a security watch.

"We've got some information that your Air Wing Commander might be interested in," Ford explained. "Can you take us to him right away?"

"Certainly, Captain," the pilot answered. "In fact he's just as anxious to see you. We have orders to escort you directly to his office."

When Ford was ushered into the presence of the Wing Commander, he felt as if he was meeting Sir Harry again. Except for the fact that this officer sported a luxuriant red moustache, the stance and demeanor reminded him of his last meeting with a British Colonial official.

"Captain Ford," the Commander extended his hand. "Good to see you. You had a smooth flight, I trust?"

Ford shook the extended hand. "Smooth enough, considering the weather we ran into. But we did come across something I think you will be interested in."

"Oh, yes? And what would that be, Captain?"

"Just about an hour before landing we were down around 300 feet to get below the cloud base and we ran smack across the top of a Japanese submarine as it was surfacing. My navigator got a fairly good fix at the time and we think you ought to check it out. Here is the position we estimated for the contact." He reached into his pocket and brought out the small sheet of paper with the coordinates written on it.

The Wing Commander smiled slightly as he took the paper from Ford's hand. "Japanese submarine in our local waters?" he mused, almost to himself. "Highly unlikely, I should think. We've maintained constant patrols around the island and well into the Bay of Bengal. Haven't had any sighting of such activity. Are you sure it was a submarine and not one of our local fishing boats?"

"As sure as we could be from 300 feet. Even spotted them unlimbering their deck gun for a shot at us. But we managed to climb back into the cloud cover before they could get a good bead on us."

The Commander seemed reluctant to accept Ford's report of the encounter. "Identification of vessels on the surface is a highly specialized skill, Captain. If there were enemy submarines in the area I'm sure our boys would know about it. Is it possible that what you saw was a local fishing boat? Some of them have been armed with small caliber guns as protection against hostile vessels. Perhaps they did not recognize you as a friendly craft. That would explain why they fired at you."

The officer's reluctance to accept the report as accurate annoyed Ford. This 'Colonel Blimp' is an idiot, Ford thought, you'd think he'd be happy to have this information. Oh, well, it's his war, not mine. "Well, sir," he sighed, "you can believe what you like. I and my crew know what we saw. Right now I'm too tired to argue about it. You're welcome to use it or not as you see fit. As for me, I would just like to get myself and my crew billeted down for some rest. We've still a long way to go and we have to see about refueling our ship. By the way, can we get aviation grade 100 octane here? We had to run on 90 octane auto gas most of the way from Surabaya and I'm not sure that has done our engines any good."

With the change of subject, the Commander became more amenable. "Why, yes, I believe we can accommodate you in that regard. I'll have the order cut right away and you can arrange for the refueling to begin this afternoon."

"One other thing, if I may, Commander," Ford added, "is there any chance we can pick up some navigation charts? We've been doing a lot of makeshift flight planning ever since we left Noumea and it would be helpful if we could get charts that would allow us to plot our course more accurately."

"I would recommend that you contact the Command Headquarters at Colombo. They would be the best source for charts. If you wish, I can arrange for a car and driver. It's about a three or four hour drive to the other side of the island."

Ford mulled over this information. He was dead tired from lack of sleep, but he knew the importance of accurate navigation. He decided quickly. "Yes, the car and driver sound fine. When can we go?"

"This afternoon if you wish."

"Good. I'll bring my Second Officer, Rod Brown, with me. First Officer Johnny Mack will have to remain on board the ship – Company security policy – and if you could find billeting for the rest of the crew..."

"Of course, Captain," the officer assured him. "Everything will be taken care of. I'll send the car and driver over to pick you up at the BOQ[8] at 1400 hours. And I'll send a dispatch ahead to alert them that you are coming."

With refueling and billeting arranged for, Ford and the rest of the crew were escorted to the RAF transient bachelor quarters. Most of them sought out their beds immediately; but Ford and Rod Brown

---

[8] BOQ: Bachelor Officers' Quarters

had no chance to get much rest. Promptly at 2 P.M. the car and driver arrived to take them to Colombo.

CHAPTER XII
A SPECIAL INVITATION

The sun was setting as the Jeep entered the Command Headquarters compound at Colombo, at that time the capital of Ceylon, a province of Britain's Indian Empire. After the war it would become a separate dominion, and renamed Sri Lanka. After confirming their identity with the sentry, they were directed to the RAF Section where Ford and Brown obtained the necessary navigation charts for the flight legs to Africa. As they were getting ready for the long drive back to Trincomalee they were approached by a liaison officer from the Commander's office.

"Captain Ford," the young lieutenant explained, "I have been directed to relay to you an invitation to supper at the Commander's residence. They have been looking forward to meeting you ever since getting word of your flight from Surabaya."

"Oh," Ford demurred, "that's very generous, but I'm sure we're not very presentable in our present condition. We've had very little sleep and we've been living in these clothes 'round the clock."

"No problem, sir," the lieutenant explained. "The dinner party is not until 2100 hours. We can put you up in the BOQ for a few hours sleep and arrange to have your uniforms cleaned and pressed in time for you to attend. They are quite eager to meet you."

The young officer's logic was hard to refute. "I suppose we can't refuse such a persuasive invitation," Ford agreed. "By the way, who is our host?"

"I'm not at liberty to say at this time, sir, but you will be properly introduced when we escort you to the Commander's residence."

Well, Ford thought to himself, that seems to be unnecessarily mysterious, but I guess they have their reasons. "Rod," he turned to his Second Officer, "it seems we have an invitation we can't refuse. And I can tell you, the offer of that BOQ bunk for a few hours sleep sounds mighty good right now."

"Sounds good to me, too, Skipper," Brown answered.

The Lieutenant directed them to the BOQ where they were each assigned a small room. An orderly took their uniforms. After a brief but welcome bath, each of them turned in for as much sleep as they could get before the dinner party. They had been sleeping less than three hours when the orderly returned with their freshly cleaned and pressed uniforms. He informed them that their driver was waiting to take them to the Commander's residence.

When they arrived at the Commander's quarters they were ushered into a large entry hall. Several orderlies were standing just inside the door. At the center of the entry stood a very stately, formally dressed woman. She smiled cordially and extended her hand as Ford and Brown walked in. The sight took them by surprise. After many days of dealing with drab, uniformed men, the appearance of this attractive, fashionably dressed lady was somewhat of a shock.

"Captain Ford," she greeted them, "so good of you to accept our invitation. We have been looking forward to meeting you."

Ford shook her extended hand and nodded slightly. "Thank you, ma'am for the invitation. But you have me at a disadvantage. I'm afraid we've not had the pleasure of meeting before."

"Forgive me, Captain," the woman explained, "but I thought the lieutenant had informed you," and she shot an inquisitive glance at the officer who had brought them in. "I am Lady Wavell. My husband is General Archibald Percival Wavell, Commander in Chief of the China-Burma-India theater of operations.[9] Unfortunately, he has been called away on pressing war matters, but he has asked me to represent him as host for this evening."

---

[9] Albert S. Tucker, Jr., *Pacific Clipper – The Untold Story*, The News-Gazette Print Shop 2001, page 83, note 8. This corrects information in the original version of *The Long Way Home* in which the identity of Ford's dinner hostess is reported as Lady Mountbatten. Mr. Tucker's research revealed that Lord Mountbatten did not take command of the China-Burma-India theater until 1943 – well after Ford's visit. Thanks to Al Tucker for correcting this detail of the story.

"Well, it's a pleasure to meet you, Lady Wavell," Ford responded in his best 'Company PR' manner. "And this is my Second Officer, Rod Brown."

"Mr. Brown," Lady Wavell extended her hand again. "Very happy to meet you." The two shook hands. "Now we are almost ready to go in to dinner," she continued, "but I would like to ask a favor of you."

"Anything at all," Ford responded.

"Ever since we received word of your flight, my son has been eager to meet you. Your flying Clipper is perhaps more famous than you realize. And the thought of you taking it around the world has created quite a stir of interest. Would it be too much to ask if you could meet him for just a few minutes before we dine? It's quite a bit past his normal bedtime, but we promised to allow him to stay up if you would see him."

"It would be our pleasure, ma'am."

With Lady Wavell leading the way, Ford, Brown, and one of the orderlies proceeded toward the rear of the residence where they entered a small bedroom. Seated on the bed was a young boy who could not have been more than five or six years old. Lady Wavell sat down next to him and put her arm around his shoulder.

"Look, my dear," she said, "here are the Clipper pilots come to see you. Now what do you think of that?"

The boy looked up wide-eyed at the two men. Ford approached, smiling, and knelt down in front of him. "Hello there, young man," he said, extending his hand. "Very pleased to make your acquaintance."

The child hesitated a moment.

"Shake hands, dear," Lady Wavell prompted him. "We must mind our manners."

The boy took Ford's outstretched hand and seemed to relax a bit. "Are you really flying around the world?" he asked.

"Yes, we are, but we still have a long way to go."

"I wish I could fly 'round the world," he responded with more enthusiasm, "it must be ever so much fun."

"Well, sometimes it's fun but mostly it's a lot of hard work. But I'm sure you'll be a fine pilot when you grow up. Just remember when you start school to keep on studying hard and learn all you can. That's the best way to get to do whatever you want. Even fly around the world."

"Can I see your aeroplane?"

"Well, it's over on the other side of the island at Trincomalee. I'm afraid there won't be much time for that before we leave in the morning."

"And now it is really bedtime," Lady Wavell interjected. "Would-be pilots must get their full ration of sleep, so off with you."

The boy looked up at Ford and they shook hands again. Then Lady Wavell kissed her son goodnight and turned him over to the ministrations of the nanny who had been waiting to one side. She led Ford and Brown back to the dining room.

The ensuing meal amounted to a state dinner with the British VIP brass who were eager to meet and talk to the Pan American pilots.

Despite his apparent celebrity status, Ford was hard put to hold up his end of the dinner conversation. The short nap he had been able to take earlier had not relieved the fatigue of the last few days. Several times during the course of the meal he felt himself being nudged by Rod Brown, having dozed off right in the middle of some polite dinner conversation. If Lady Wavell or any of the other guests noticed it, they were too courteous to mention it. In this way they managed to get through the evening. When it was over and the last thank-yous and handshakes were tendered, both of them were grateful for the opportunity to return to the BOQ for a longer rest. The return to Trincomalee was arranged for the next morning.

The harbor at Trincomalee was calm as Bob Ford pushed the throttles forward for full power takeoff. The quiet of the Christmas Eve morning was shattered by the roar of the engines as NC18602 surged forward into the takeoff run. Their destination was Karachi. It took almost a minute to become airborne. They had loaded 4,000 gallons of aviation fuel the night before, but there was still some auto gas in the inboard main tanks. Both Ford and Swede Rothe counted on the enrichment from the newly loaded 100 octane to overcome the poor detonation qualities of the leftover auto gas. As soon as they reached a safe altitude, they went through the familiar ritual of leaning out the engines for best fuel consumption. Once again they experienced the intermittent backfiring of the previous flight.

"We'll probably have to put up with that until the fuel flow purges all of that 90 octane stuff out of the system," Rothe reasoned. "We'd better monitor those cylinder head temps real close. They're still too much on the high side for my taste."

"Okay, Swede," Ford agreed. "Let's hold 2,000 feet until the fuel load lightens a bit. Then we'll see about a higher altitude."

Finally, trimmed for level flight and on course toward Karachi, they settled down into the usual routine of en route flying. They were about thirty minutes out and Ford was ready to go below for his customary cup of coffee when suddenly the aircraft was shaken by a loud explosion.

"What the hell!" Johnny Mack exclaimed.

The flying boat yawed right. Ford instinctively applied corrective rudder and aileron. As he did so he glanced out his side window toward the engines. Johnny Mack turned to inspect the engines on the starboard side. A wide, black swath of oil was streaming back from the Number Three engine.

"Number Three's lost oil pressure!" Swede Rothe called from the engineer's station. "Cutting of fuel flow, feathering Three!"

Mack watched as the big Hamilton propeller slowed, then stopped with the blades edgewise to the air stream. Then he switched off the magnetos for Number Three.

"Jocko!" Ford called to John Parrish who was standing next to the engineer's desk. "Get up to the dome and see if you can make out what's happened to Number Three."

Parrish hurried through the hatch to the rear compartment and climbed the short ladder. Glancing out of the dome, he could see the wide swath of engine oil streaming back off the wing.

"It looks like we've blown a jug," Parrish reported. "It's a real mess out there."

Ford swung the Clipper around in a 180-degree turn. "Well, that does it. We'll have to return to Trincomalee."

"We're going to get some use out of those spare parts we brought along," Johnny Mack mused.

Half an hour later they were circling back over the harbor at Trincomalee. As soon as they were secured to the seaplane dock and all engines shut down, Swede Rothe and Jocko Parrish climbed out on top of the wing and inspected the damaged engine.

"We've blown number six cylinder on the Number Three engine," Rothe reported to Ford. "Ten studs are broken. We're going to have to draw those broken studs out before we can replace the cylinder from our spare parts. Better figure on at least two days to get the job done. Merry Christmas!"

Ford half-smiled at Rothe's wry humor. "Yeah, and a Happy New Year, too. Well, let's get on it."

Rothe recruited Verne White, and the two Noumea mechanics, Bud Washer and Ralph Hitchcock to help with the repairs. Fortunately, White had brought his hand-held air drill with him from Auckland; but they did not have an air compressor or hose to hook it up to.

"Do you think the Brits might have a portable compressor and hose we can borrow?" Parrish asked.

"Why don't you get on over to their hangar and check it out," Rothe replied. "Meanwhile me and the boys will get the cowlings off and pull down the work doors." The work doors were short hinged platforms that could extend from the engine mount, allowing mechanics to work on the engines while suspended over the water. There was one on each side of each engine and when extended, the mechanics could stand on them to begin the laborious process of repairs.

A couple of hours later, Parrish returned from the British airbase. Luckily, they had the portable compressor and hose they needed. Very soon they were busy drawing the broken studs while Washer and Hitchcock prepared the spare cylinder head for installation.

The job took longer than expected. By midnight they had drawn out only about half of the ten broken studs. "Hell, I'm bushed," Rothe exclaimed. "Let's knock off and get a little shut-eye. We can get on it again in the morning. This is one helluva lousy way to spend Christmas Eve."

With Jocko Parrish and Bob Henricksen assigned on-board security watch for the night, the rest of the crew went ashore. The RAF pilots invited them to a Christmas Eve party but they politely declined in favor of a good night's sleep. Time enough for celebrations when they got the engine repaired.

By noon the last of the broken studs were removed from the engine and a new cylinder installed. The ignition harness was repaired, fuel and oil lines checked and Number Three oil tank was replenished from a barrel of spare engine oil. When all was cleaned up and secured, Rothe approached Ford.

"Well, Skipper," he said, "that ought to do it. We can fly again whenever you're ready."

"Good work, Swede," Ford complimented his engineer, "but I think we'll have to put off departure until tomorrow. We need to arrive at Karachi in daylight and as that leg appears to be only about nine hours, an early morning departure would be best. We need to top the tanks again and that will take some time. Besides, we might as well relax. After all, it is Christmas."

"Yeah, and what a helluva way to spend it!" Rothe responded.

Leaving the mandatory two crew members on board as a security watch, Ford and the rest of the crew went ashore. For the rest of the evening and that night they tried to relax and rest. The RAF fighter pilots were throwing a big Christmas party at the officer' mess and, for a while, they joined in the festivities.

But for most of the Pan Am crew their thoughts were directed toward home and family. Especially Jack Poindexter. The other crew members' families had expected them to be gone for the usual long flight duty associated with the run to New Zealand. But Poindexter and his family were caught totally unprepared for his sudden and extended absence. He wondered if there was any way to send a message home, at least just to say that he was well and everything was okay. But inquiries through the RAF officers proved fruitless. Not even the British pilots could send messages home. And some of them had been away at Christmas each year for the past three years. Wartime security was simply too tight and strict. Messages home would have to wait for a more secure time and place.

Thus they passed the time on Christmas Night: swapping stories with the RAF pilots, conjecturing on the course of the war and wondering when they would be home again. When they tired of the drinking and story swapping they retired to their quarters to rest up for the morning departure: another venture into the unknown; another day of flying where they had never flown before.

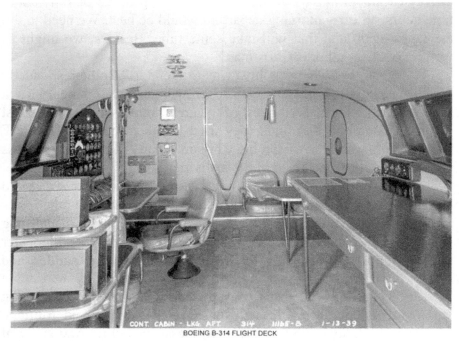

CONT. CABIN - LKG AFT. 314 1165-8 1-13-39
BOEING B-314 FLIGHT DECK

B314 flight deck looking aft. Hatches on the left and right bulkheads led to passageways into the wing with access to each engine in flight. The door on rear bulkhead led to the aft cargo area and access to the navigator's dome where celestial navigation by star sightings was performed.

CHAPTER XIII
TOURISTS IN A STRANGE LAND

John Steers was taking his turn in the right seat. Four hours ago they had crossed the coast of India. From their altitude of 7,500 feet, Steers looked down at the unfamiliar landscape, trying to make a connection between major landmarks on the ground and the information on the newly-acquired flight charts that Ford had obtained at Colombo.

They were passing over badly eroded open hill country interspersed with occasional patches of green terraces. Once, he sighted what appeared to be a beautiful castle. It gleamed white against the dull brown of the mountain top on which it was perched. But Steers could not find it on the map. It sat alone, in pristine isolation, with no village or town within miles. Hmm, he mused to himself, a prominent landmark like that ought to be marked on this chart, but damned if I can find it. Oh, well, it's a good thing we have the coastline just off there to the west. That's a good enough surface reference for a direct course to Karachi.

Soon they passed over Bombay. By 4 P.M. they were landing in the harbor at Karachi. The nine and a half hour flight was one of the smoothest and least eventful legs thus far. Perhaps there would be time now to relax and shed the tensions of the past few days and look forward to an uneventful conclusion to their odyssey.

There was one major chore, however, that had to be undertaken before they could be on their way. The engine taken on at Auckland had to be off-loaded. The Allied Command was building a forward airbase and the engine was to be added to the inventory of the new base. Once again the navigator's hatch was opened. Very gingerly, the crane operator lowered the hook and cable into the opening. With Swede Rothe assisting, they raised the bulky cargo out of the cargo area and placed it on the dock. Well, Rothe thought to himself, this will relieve some of our load problems. Ought be able to take on more gas with that thing out of our hair.

In addition to off-loading the engine, Ford reminded Verne White that he was to deplane at Karachi and accompany the engine and its spare parts to the new base where he would be in charge of setting up the new engine maintenance shop. Bud Washer and Ralph Hitchcock were to remain with Ford until they got to Bahrain, where they would deplane to take up a similar assignment there. All three would remain at their new duty stations for almost two months before being picked up by Pan Am Captain Masland, in another B-314, for their eventual return to the U.S.

With the engine unloading completed and the security watch established for the evening, the rest of the crew went ashore and checked into the Carlton Hotel. The first thing that most of them did was to take advantage of the deep bathtubs. It felt good to soak away the sweat and grime. Steers lay back, closed his eyes and luxuriated in the unaccustomed pleasure of the full tub. When he had soaked enough, he reached down and pulled the drain plug. The water ran out all over the floor. "Oh, for Christ sake!" he muttered aloud. It seemed the builders had installed the tubs and then neglected to hook up any plumbing drains. Steers had to laugh as he tip-toed away from the flooded floor, toweled off, and got dressed.

Bob Ford awoke early and returned to the dock where NC18602 lay moored. "What's the word on refueling, Swede?"

Swede and Jocko Parrish had spent the night on board in anticipation of an early morning start. "No problem there, Skipper, but there is something else that will need fixing before we can fly again."

Ford frowned, "Oh, and what might that be?"

"Jocko and I were checking the engines earlier. During one of the routine prop checks on Number Three we hit what looks like a stuck propeller pitch control piston[10] We'll have to change it."

"Damn!" Ford swore, "How long?"

"At least a day. Depends on what we find when we open it up."

---

[10] The blades on the variable-pitch propellers were adjusted by a set of pistons built into the control located in the hub of the propeller.

Ford sighed, "Well, get on it pronto. I'll let the rest of the crew know. They can relax and get in some sight-seeing for the rest of the day."

Ford returned to the Carlton where the other crew members were finishing breakfast. "You can take it easy for today, boys," he announced. "Swede says we need to change a prop control piston. Could be an all-day job. We'll aim for an early departure tomorrow morning."

For their part, the rest of the crew seemed happy to have a short break from the demands of their harried flight schedule. It would be an opportunity to attend to some long overdue personal matters, such as laundering their clothes and catching up on sleep. For those so inclined, it was also a chance to explore a strange city which none of them had ever been to before and which they would probably never see again. John Steers, Jack Poindexter, Barney Sawicki, and Eugene Leach opted to take a leisurely stroll around the city. It soon became a first-hand lesson in cultural differences.

The streets were crowded with people. Shopkeepers called to them as they passed and they were continually accosted by peddlers trying to sell them all sorts of overpriced goods. Everywhere they strolled there was a pervasive odor. After a while they decided it was the camel dung in the streets where the passing animals had deposited it and where it lay putrefying in the hot sun. Then there were the beggars. Hordes of ill-dressed, pitiful creatures surrounded them as they went; pawing at them and pleading for money. The women were most persistent; even those nursing babies and breast feeding them were reaching out to these strangers in hopes of getting a handout. But they had nothing to give. Their personal funds had been exhausted by now and they were all dependent on the meager funds remaining from the money Bob Ford had been able to glean from company funds at Auckland and the money he had obtained at Gladstone. All they could do was shrug and fend off the pawing hordes as best they could. After a couple of hours of this, they returned to the relative calm and quiet of the Carlton. The rest of the day and evening was spent playing cards, reading, or engaging in speculative bull sessions at the bar. Most of them turned in early, looking forward to an early departure for the next flight leg to Bahrain.

The fuel tanks were topped off with 3,100 gallons of aviation fuel. In the early morning stillness of December 28th, NC18602 lifted off from Karachi harbor. Ford took up a westerly heading paralleling the coastline along the north shore of the Gulf of Oman. Soon they crossed the Strait of Hormuz and entered the Persian Gulf. A little over eight uneventful hours out of Karachi they landed at the Arabian port of Bahrain. Once secured at a seaplane dock, they emerged from the cabin into the hottest, most humid air any of them had experienced since leaving Auckland.

"Phew!" Swede Rothe exclaimed, as the moist blanket of air hit him in the face. "Let's gas up and get out of here. This place would sweat the cooties off a hound dog."

"Well, Swede," Ford responded, "I'm all for that, but I guess we're stuck till morning. We're going to have to land on the Nile River when we get to Khartoum and I'd sure rather do it in daylight."

As soon as they could, they contacted the local commander to arrange for refueling. To their dismay, they learned that there was no 100 octane available and they would have to fall back on the less desirable auto gas.

"Here we go again!" Rothe exclaimed.

"It's either that or sit here for the duration," Ford replied.

"Yeah, I know. Well, we've nursed these mothers this far. I guess we can do it again as long as they'll hold up. I'm sure not much for hanging around this Turkish bath weather any longer than we have to."

Fortunately, the flight from Karachi had used up only about half of their fuel capacity. They would only have to top off with the auto gas. The mixing of the two octanes might not be as harmful as the first time, when they had been forced to use an almost 100 percent supply of the 90 octane. Once again John Steers stayed on board to help Rothe with the refueling. The rest of the crew went ashore and settled in for the night. As promised, and as they had been notified earlier, the two flight mechanics from Noumea deplaned at Bahrain.

When Bob Ford came out of the hotel the next morning he was surprised to find the streets running with water. That's strange, he thought, I didn't hear any rain last night or this morning. Wonder where all this water is coming from. After some local inquiry, it turned out that it was dew. The high humidity coupled with overnight cooling had served to condense so much moisture out of the air that the gutters ran with water as though there had been a heavy rainstorm. But he did not have much time to dwell on the phenomenon. Mostly he was concerned about the engines. Would this second load of auto gas raise more havoc than the first? How would they manage if other cylinders blew under the stress of the higher head temperatures? They would just have to chance it. Later, as he filed his flight plan with the British air controller, another problem arose.

The British dispatcher looked at Ford and chose his words carefully. "Captain, I don't know if you are aware of it, but there is a very strict prohibition against aircraft flying over the Arabian Peninsula. Your flight plan for a direct flight to Khartoum can not be approved as filed, as it would take you directly over Mecca. You will have to proceed north until you reach Kuwait before you can turn west. The Saudis are very sensitive to any incursions into air space overlying their sacred areas."

Ford shrugged. "Whatever works. Just get us clearance."

Just before takeoff Ford huddled with Rod Brown. "Rod, the British say we can't go direct, so we have to head north for a while. Refigure a course and estimate until we can decide when it will be safe to head west."

Once at altitude, Swede Rothe attempted to lean out the mixtures, only to produce the by-now familiar popping and backfiring as the engines protested against the diet of lower octane fuel. Using an optimum setting to minimize the backfiring, they settled into a cruising altitude of 10,000 feet which took them above a solid undercast of clouds. Ford contemplated the broad cloud deck below and then made a decision.

"What the hell!" he announced. "With this undercast they'll never know we're up here. Let's get back to our original course. I doubt that they have any way to detect our presence."

With that, he swung the Boeing around and headed west-southwest to pick up their original course. With the engines popping occasionally, they continued above the clouds. In a few hours they were almost across the Arabian Peninsula. Then the clouds began to break up. Just as they came into the clear, Johnny Mack looked down and saw an unusual sight. They were flying directly over the Great Mosque at Mecca. Thousands of people – looking like ants swarming out of an ant hill – were streaming out of the Mosque and hundreds of flashes of light were appearing. "Hey, Bob, I do believe those folks are shooting at us!"

Ford looked down also. "I don't think that'll do them much good. Looks like mostly rifle fire of some kind. Can't possibly reach us at this altitude."

"Just as long as these engines keep going. I'd hate to be down there amongst them right now."

Mecca receded slowly behind them and soon was lost to view in the tropical haze. Soon they crossed the shoreline and headed across the Red Sea. By late afternoon they had intercepted the Nile and followed it to Khartoum, where they landed in the river. While the crew remained on board, Ford went ashore in a dinghy to hunt up the British commander and arrange once again for refueling. "Swede, you check those engines thoroughly while we're here. No telling how much damage that lousy auto gas has done. I know we can get avgas at Leopoldville, but we still have to get out of here. I'm going to check around for avgas. When you're done checking the engines, you and the rest of the crew remain on board until I can see to our overnight accommodations."

Fortunately, Ford found that 100 octane aviation fuel was readily available, and he arranged for refueling for the next day. The RAF provided him with charts covering the entire route from Khartoum to Leopoldville. They would no longer be dependent on the makeshift atlases and maps they had obtained at Auckland. While at the British dispatch office, Ford was approached by the dispatcher.

"Captain Ford, we have received a dispatch from Command Headquarters at Cairo, requesting that you wait here for a VIP passenger coming in via BOAC who will be going to Leopoldville with you. The BOAC aircraft is expected to arrive some time in the next day or two."

"You mean we're being ordered to wait here?"

"Yes, I'm afraid so. It seems you are the only available transport from here to Leopoldville at this time."

Ford sighed. "I hope he's 'VIP' enough to justify delaying us like this. We'd sure like to get away as soon as possible and get this damn trip over with!"

"I can understand your concern, Captain," the dispatcher tried to be conciliatory, "but we have these orders from Command headquarters in Cairo. Can't very well ignore them."

"No, I suppose not. Well, can you at least arrange for some decent accommodations for my crew? They might as well relax and enjoy themselves if they have to sit around here twiddling their thumbs for a couple of days."

The dispatcher assured him that overnight accommodations would be forthcoming. He arranged for billeting at the Grand Hotel.

Ford returned to the ship to break the news to the crew and bring them ashore for the night.

"Damn! What a waste of time!" Johnny Mack exclaimed in disgust. He had just heard about the arrival of the VIP passenger they had waited two days to receive. "She's no more a VIP than I am!"

It turned out that the so-called VIP passenger was the wife of a minor British supply officer who had fast-talked her way onto the VIP passenger list for transport to Leopoldville.

Ford tried to placate him. "It's water under the bridge now, Johnny. Let's just get on with it and get the hell out of here as soon as possible. Once we reach Leopoldville we'll be back in Company territory and that should count for something toward finishing up this little detour of ours."

The rest of New Year's Eve day was spent refueling. For a time it looked as if they would not be able to take on a full load of fuel because of the very short seaplane channel area marked off along the Nile. A full gross load would require a longer takeoff run.

"This chart shows that the marked channel for seaplane operations is only 1,300 yards long," Swede Rothe explained. "The only way we can get airborne in that distance is to lighten up our load and the only way we can do that is to limit the amount of gas we take aboard. We'll never make it to Leopoldville that way and we'd have to find an intermediate stop to refuel."

Ford studied the chart. "What are the chances we could use a longer area – go outside the marked seaplane channel?"

"Chancy, Skipper. We'd have to set up a special sweep to make sure we have an obstruction-free zone. Might take a while and I don't know if there is that much clear area outside the charted channel."

"Let's find out. I'd just as soon take on a full load of gas and go direct to Leopoldville."

John Steers had been listening closely to this conversation. "Hell, Skipper, I saw where the Limey boys have a small speedboat tied up at that small dock. I think we could get them to take us out to survey the area. It shouldn't take too long to find out if we've got a long enough clearway for a full-gross takeoff."

"Okay, do it."

In a few minutes John Steers, two British soldiers, and a couple of Egyptian river pilots, were all motoring up the Nile looking for a likely takeoff channel that would be long enough. With the river chart on his lap, Steers marked off distances as they searched for hidden sand bars, rocks, or other obstructions that might be in the way. Finally, after about forty minutes, he had traced a clear channel three miles long. "That should do it," he called to the river pilots. "Let's head back."

By the time they got back to the Boeing it was getting dark. Ford looked at the area on Steers' chart. "If you're sure of those marks, that should be okay for full-gross takeoff. Let's get on with the refueling. But I think we should all spend the night here. That way we can start in the morning at first light."

On New Year's Day, 1942, NC18602 surged forward as Bob Ford held the throttles full open and concentrated his gaze toward the far end of the three mile takeoff area that John Steers had marked on the chart. I hope John didn't miss any obstructions, Ford thought, as he watched the dirty yellow river water rush past the bow. This sure isn't the time to get hung up on a tree snag or sandbar.

The Wright engines seemed to be running smoothly today. The steady roar was reassuring, after all the trouble the 90 octane auto gas had caused. Ford glanced at the airspeed. As it hit 70 knots he started his usual rocking motion on the yoke to break the big hull free of the water. The slap of the water stopped abruptly as the big machine came unstuck and started to climb. Just as abruptly there was a loud popping noise and the smooth roar of the engines was joined by a new sound. A rapid, pulsating hammering.

"What the hell is that!" Ford exclaimed. "Swede, what gives?"

"Don't know, Skipper," Rothe called out. "All gauges show normal. Still a little high on head temps, but no power loss." He turned to Jocko Parrish. "High-tail it up to the navigator's dome and check the engines from there."

Parrish hurried through the hatch to the rear baggage area, climbed the ladder, scanned the tops of the engine cowling, and took only a second to see what had happened. Quickly he returned to the flight deck. "Number One has lost the aft section of its exhaust stack. It must have blown loose. That exhaust plume is streaming out right over the wing surface."

Rothe relayed the report to Ford.

Ford swore. "Now what? Swede, can we fly this way?"

"Engine gauges are good. We're not losing power. In fact we're still climbing. I think you can throttle back to standard cruise climb now."

136

Ford eased back on the throttles and the Boeing settled into its standard 500 feet-per-minute climb. He glanced quickly out his side window toward the damaged engine. He could see nothing wrong. The broken exhaust stack was above the wing, out of his line of vision. The only evidence of its condition was the constant hammering noise that was now just one part of the mixture of engine sounds filling the flight deck

"Want to turn back and land?" Johnny Mack asked.

"I don't know what good that'd do," Ford reasoned. "No spare parts here and we don't have a spare exhaust stack on board. There's just no way we can fix it here. What's the risk of flying with it as is?"

"It jacks up the fire hazard odds," Rothe explained. "If we're lucky it shouldn't affect engine performance any. Just makes it damn noisy."

Ford mulled this over for a few seconds. Then he decided. "We'll go on. Post a man in the navigation dome and keep a constant watch on that engine. Swede, stay on those temperature gauges. The only way we're going to turn back now is if that engine fails completely. As long as it's putting out rated power we'll use it. Now let's all settle in and tend to business."

As soon as they left the Nile Valley they were over open, rolling hill country. There were only a few villages in what appeared to be an empty vastness. Continuing south, they passed a range of low hills and the vegetation became denser. Soon they were flying over a green carpet of the African tropical forest, interspersed with small streams and the occasional road. After a few hours the vegetation was so dense that it hid the landmarks they were trying to use for navigation. For a long while they had to fall back on dead reckoning, hoping the winds would not take them too far off course. Finally, they sighted the Congo River, whose sheer size made it unmistakable, and descended low enough to follow it toward Leopoldville. The coffee-colored water stood out boldly against the jungle growth on all sides. Ten hours and 23 minutes out of Khartoum, Ford lined up as best he could on the winding river and eased the big ship onto the surface. As the Boeing slowed and settled, Ford felt the tug of the river current. He had thought it to be a sluggish current when viewed from the air. But the flow was much stronger. Ford estimated that the river was running at about six knots. They would have to find a secure anchorage.

Pan American was just beginning to build its African bases when the war came along. The one at Leopoldville was still in its early phases of construction. As a result, the facilities were still somewhat limited. Ford discovered that they would not be able to repair the broken exhaust stack. The spare parts inventory had not as yet been established. They would have to endure the hammering engine until they reached Natal. The only good news was that the supply of aviation fuel was plentiful. They would no longer be plagued by the poor performance of the 90 octane auto gas. Ford arranged for refueling and then he and the crew went ashore and checked into the Grand Hotel to snatch what sleep they could. It was the hottest, muggiest climate they had experienced thus far and the netting over their beds did little to protect them from the swarms of mosquitoes that managed to find their way through.

"Just count the bites," John Steers advised, wryly. "Then you can figure out how many scotch and sodas you'll need to counteract them. One each ought to do the job!"

CHAPTER XIV
ACROSS THE ATLANTIC

"If we top brimful on all tanks, Swede, how much over allowable gross weight would we be?" Ford queried his chief engineer.

Swede Rothe pondered the question. The normal gross weight of 82,500 pounds was based upon a carefully calculated compromise of the allocation of fuel, cargo, passengers, and the length of the flight.

This leg from Leopoldville to Natal, Brazil, would be the longest flight leg the Clipper had ever covered: 3,100 nautical miles, most of it over open ocean.[11] There would be no place to refuel if they went below the allowable reserve supply. And if they had to use up the reserve they would have to consider a forced landing at sea. The Boeing might survive the landing, but it was never designed for extended surface operations on the open ocean. Ocean waves and wind would most likely make short work of the ship and they would then find themselves adrift in the inflatable life rafts, hoping for a rescue that might or might not come. Passengers posed no problem as there were none on board. The collection of spare engine parts scattered throughout the lower cabin added some additional weight but the big unknown was how much fuel to take aboard, considering the length of the proposed flight, the possible headwinds, and the conditions for a safe landing.

"Well, Skipper," Rothe replied, "it's possible to load as much as 5,100 gallons of fuel on board. But that would put us about 2,000 pounds over gross, even without any passengers or spare parts. If we

---

[11] At the time, the base at Fisherman's Lake in Liberia had not yet been established.

were taking off in a cold climate with real low temperatures I'd say it would be no problem, but this damned heat plays hell with density altitude[12]. We'd need a helluva long takeoff channel to get off."

Ford pondered this advice. "This river is pretty long. There's not really any high terrain to clear after takeoff. What do you think?"

Rothe shrugged. "If we have no engine glitches and we can get off within the full-power parameters, I'd say let's go for it."

"Okay then, you get those tanks topped brim-full and we'll get out of this hell hole as soon as you're done."

It was midday before all the fuel was loaded. The crew had come on board earlier and now most of them were eager to get going. The stifling heat and humidity made the flight deck feel like a Turkish bath; and the sooner they could get to altitude with cooler air circulating through the cabin, the better they would like it. But before they could go Ford had to consider one other factor that would affect the takeoff.

When they had landed the day before, he had noted the strong current running in the Congo. The downstream flow was about six knots. The light breeze was blowing downstream also, at about four knots. He could elect to take off upstream, against the wind, but that would give him a six knot drag from the current. This could pose a problem when it came time to haul the big flying boat off the water. If he took off downstream, he would lose the four knot airspeed advantage, but pick up a six knot push from the current that would help get the hull out of the water. After considering the alternatives, Ford made his decision. They would take off downstream.

"Okay, Johnny," he turned to Johnny Mack, "we taxi upstream as far as the next bend in the river. Then we take off downstream. With this heat, I'm thinking we'd get a better advantage from the six knot current than from the four knot headwind."

"Downstream it is then," Mack agreed.

The temperature was hovering around the 100 degree mark. Everyone was wringing wet with sweat as they took their places on the flight deck. With all engines started and bow lines cast off, Ford shoved the throttles forward, swung around and headed upstream.

---

[12] Density Altitude: An indirect measure of air density based upon temperature, humidity, and true altitude above sea level. High temperature combined with high humidity increases density altitude. This reduces the lifting efficiency of the wing and reduces engine and propeller efficiency thereby making it more difficult to takeoff and climb.

When they reached the first bend he swung around again. Immediately he could feel the current carrying them downstream.

"Let's not waste time, Swede. Full takeoff power, NOW!"

The engines roared. The Number One engine, still without its exhaust stack, added the trip-hammer beat of its unmuffled power to the swelling sound. NC18602 surged forward, aided by the six knot current. Bob Ford concentrated his gaze far ahead, down river to the start of the Congo Gorges: the series of cataracts, rapids, and waterfalls amidst a jumbled maze of canyons and rocks, where the river began a steeper descent toward the sea. They would have to be airborne well before reaching that drop-off point. If not... Ford preferred not to think about it.

With his left hand pressing the throttles hard against the full power stops, his right hand grasping the yoke, and his eyes concentrating on the river ahead, he mentally measured the rapidly decreasing distance to the gorge.

Below, in the main cabin, Second Engineer John Parrish watched as the spray whipped over the sea wing. He was aware that the aircraft was well over normal gross weight, and mentally counted the seconds toward what he knew was the maximum allowable time for a full-power takeoff: ninety seconds. Twenty seconds went by. Thirty seconds. Still no liftoff. The spray continued to fly past his window. The surface of the river was just as close as ever. Hell! He thought, get this mother up on the step! With every passing second he had visions of the big ship running off the edge of the gorge, smashing into the rocks. He wondered how big an explosion 5,100 gallons of 100 octane fuel would make. Subconsciously he cinched his seat belt tighter and stiffened his body against what he thought might be the impact and the final moments of his life.

Bob Ford glanced quickly at the airspeed indicator. Seventy knots – the design-rated landing/stall speed. As the airspeed needle crept above that mark he gently brought the wheel back. The Clipper's bow rose above the horizon but it did not break off the water. He let the wheel forward again. With the bow down he could see the edge of the gorge 1,700 yards away. More speed, he needed more speed to break the suction. He kept the nose down, hoping to build up the airspeed.

Fifty seconds now. Sixty. Seventy. Then he decided. If we don't break off in another twenty seconds I'll pull back three engines but keep Number One at full power. Its torque will swing us around and we can head upstream. All eyes on the flight deck were fixed on the rapidly approaching gorge. No one uttered a word. Ford adjusted his grip on the throttles. He flexed his left hand. At that moment NC18602 came off the water.

But the reprieve was only momentary. They barely had flying speed and were not climbing at all; just hovering a few feet off the surface and still headed toward the gorge.

"Ninety one seconds," Swede Rothe called from the engineer's station. "That's past max time for full power. Can we pull it back now?"

"No way! Keep those throttles to the stops. We're not out of this yet!"

"Okay, but the cylinder head temps are over redline! We could blow at any time!"

Ford did not reply, but thought to himself, Hell! We'll either blow up or hit those rocks. Either way we're dead. Might as well die trying. And he kept his hand hard against the throttles. Gingerly he tested the yoke, attempting to find a balance between pulling back too far and risking a stall and maintaining just enough nose-down attitude to build up the airspeed without settling back onto the river.

At that moment they passed the rim of the gorge. The river dropped away into the rocky defile and the water turned to white foam as it crashed against the boulder-strewn bottom. Without the cushioning effect – the so-called 'ground effect' – of being only a few feet above the water surface, NC18602 also began to descend into the gorge. In seconds they were flying within the confines of a narrow canyon, still not too far above the surface. But the extra separation from the water surface did allow Ford to drop the bow a little more and gradually the airspeed began to pick up.

"Eighty five knots." Johnny Mack called out.

Okay, Ford thought, that gives us about five knots to play with to get some climb out of this baby. Gently he exerted enough back pressure on the yoke to raise the nose and drop the airspeed to eighty knots.

"Rate of climb ten feet a minute, up!" Mack exclaimed. "..twenty feet, up! ...fifty feet, up! We're going to make it!"

"We're not out of the woods yet, Johnny," Ford cautioned. "Look up ahead there."

Directly ahead the gorge took a curve to the right. They were still below the edge of the precipice and the rocky ledge loomed before them. "There seems to be room to make a shallow turn and follow the canyon."

"Yeah, as long as we don't bank too far. We're still marginal for a stall."

Ford watched the approaching curve in the gorge and mentally gauged the point at which to begin a gentle turn. As they reached that point he gently applied pressure to the wheel, turning it to the right, while, at the same time, feeding in a light pressure on the right rudder pedal. The wheel would not move. He increased pressure. The yoke would not budge. He could move it forward and back but he could not get it to turn. With no aileron movement and the slight amount of right rudder, the ship skidded left.

"Now what the hell is wrong?" he exclaimed. "Hey, Swede, we've got no aileron control. The damn wheel wont budge! What gives?"

Swede Rothe made a quick assessment: "The aileron cables must be jammed, Hang on! I'll check it out."

He rose from his seat and went to the starboard hatch leading into the wing. He opened it, peered into the tunnel, and saw the problem immediately. Looking out along the catwalk tunnel, he could se that it had a tilt to it, only slight, but noticeable to his trained eye. Then he turned his attention to the aileron cable running through the channels in the wing. At a point where the cable went through a pulley it was clamped tightly between the groove of the pulley wheel and the pulley housing. Quickly he returned to his station.

"Skipper, the aileron cables are jammed in their pulleys because the wing is flexing. We're going to have to get up into cooler air before those pulleys will free up."

As Ford digested this news from Rothe he was, at the same time, trying to improvise some way to make the big ship follow the twists and turns of the gorge. After some experimentation he found he could use the rudder by itself to skid around the turns. Each time he applied right rudder the ship would skid left and the right wing would dip down. Conversely, it worked the same when he attempted left rudder. In this way they continued: airspeed just above stall, gaining about fifty feet per minute, following the curves of the gorge.

Slowly the flying boat was able to gain enough height to put them above the surrounding terrain. Ford was eventually able to let up enough on the yoke to build up a little more airspeed. Finally they had a safe altitude and Ford called to Rothe to throttle back to normal cruise climb. The four engines had been held at full power for a full three minutes; far longer than the engineers at Wright had ever designed them for.

"By God, I don't want to try that again any time soon!" Rothe exclaimed to no one in particular.

As the tension eased and NC18602 approached its normal cruising altitude, Ford relaxed a little. But he listened carefully to the engines. Except for the hammering of Number One, they all sounded good. Well, he thought, I guess they're none the worse for wear. But that was too close!

Satisfied that the engines had not suffered any damage from the extended time at full power, Ford called to Rod Brown for a compass heading to Natal. When the customary small slip of paper with the heading written on it was taped to the brow of the instrument panel, he turned the Clipper westward, heading toward the South Atlantic and what he hoped would be the final episode in this strange odyssey.

Midnight: clear and smooth as NC18602 continued westward. They were half-way across the South Atlantic. Earlier they had been forced to take a northwesterly course to avoid several lines of thunderstorms that lay just off the African coast. Second Officer Rod Brown was now taking several star sightings to determine their position and make the necessary course correction to return to the direct track to Natal. As he took his readings and plotted them on the Mercator chart, he could see that winds aloft had pushed them much further north of their intended track. They would have to make a considerable heading change. He had better huddle with Parrish, he thought, to see what the Howgozit Curve[13] said about their fuel reserves.

"Jocko, these fixes indicate strong southerly upper winds. We're going to have to take a pretty hefty dog-leg cut at our compass heading to get back on track. I'd say we're looking at least at an additional two to three hours added to our original flight time. What does the curve say about our fuel reserves?"

Parrish studied the Howgozit line on the chart. Then he took his ruler and penciled in a tentative extension based on the new

---

[13] Howgozit Curve: A line plotted on the navigation chart to measure fuel consumption against flight progress. Used to determine, at any point in a flight, if there is enough fuel to reach destination with a suitable reserve for emergencies.

position plot. "Well, it's going to be tight. If we slow down to a minimum long-range cruise, I reckon we can make Natal with about a two-hour reserve. That is if these upper winds don't play any more tricks on us."

"Don't count on it. All this damned wartime secrecy and radio silence is really lousing up our chances to get any decent weather information. I guess we'll just have to go with the wind estimates I've worked up from these star fixes. I'd better let Ford know. He might want to review ditching procedures."

Below, in the main cabin, Bob Ford, Johnny Mack, Swede Rothe and Jack Poindexter were finishing up a late meal. As Verne Edwards cleared away the last of the empty dishes, they all relaxed and took a few moments for some after-dinner conversation.

"That was one of the better meals I've had on this trip." Swede Rothe complimented the steward. "How the hell do you guys manage that?"

Ever since leaving Noumea, stewards Barney Sawicki and Verne Edwards had done a lot of creative shopping to keep the crew supplied with enough to eat. As their dollar funds ran low they had resorted to some very heavy haggling at the various marketplaces along the way. At Leopoldville they had coaxed and bargained with the cooks at the Pan American commissary until they had amassed a relatively nourishing store of groceries. "Hey," Edwards demurred, "nothing to it if you're born con-artists like we are!"

Ford turned to Jack Poindexter and grinned. "How's your shirt holding up, Jack? Think it'll make it to New York?"

Ever since his unexpected assignment out of Los Angeles, Jack Poindexter had dealt with the problem of his lack of preparation for such a long flight. With only the clothes on his back and the one extra shirt he had bought in Honolulu, he had faced the constant chore of keeping his clothes clean. Whenever possible, at each stopover point, the first thing he did was to find somewhere to wash his shirts and underwear. He had managed to have his uniform cleaned only once, during the layover at Trincomalee. By now he was really looking forward to the end of their journey and a chance to wear some decent street clothes. "It damn well better hang together 'til then!" he answered. "I'm not scrubbing another shirt for the next hundred years!"

They all laughed. For a few moments they savored the flavor of the just-finished meal.

Johnny Mack broke the silence. "I'll just be damned glad to get this over with and get back to 'Frisco. I'm just curious about what they intend to do with this ship once we're at LaGuardia."

"The best I can figure it," Ford interjected, "they plan to turn all the Clippers over to the Navy. At least that was implied in the Plan A letter. I don't know if the Navy has pilots checked out in them, but I'd be willing to bet dollars to doughnuts that we're going to find ourselves 'volunteering' for enlistment for the duration. The Navy sure as hell can't fly these babies without trained crews and as far as that goes... we're them."

All nodded in agreement. Clearly, the advent of war had changed their future. But certain givens were obvious; every effort, every plan could be directed toward only one goal: the successful conclusion of the war. If that meant they would all be inducted into the service in one way or another, then so be it. Along with every other person in the country, all their personal plans and hopes were now on hold.

Jack Poindexter also thought about his family. The last message he had been able to send was from Noumea, just before the Pearl Harbor attack. For sure, he thought, his wife would be calling the Treasure Island operations office every day to see if they had any word on his whereabouts. He wondered how she was managing; adjusting each day to the uncertainty about his safety and well-being and, because of the complete radio silence, not a single hint of his fate or whereabouts. Well, just another few days, then it will be over.

Just then Rod Brown appeared in the passageway. "Skipper, I think you should take a look at the flight progress plots. We could be running pretty close on our fuel reserves."

"Oh? How close?" Ford asked as he rose to accompany Brown to the flight deck.

"After the diversion we took to get around those two lines of thunderstorms, it looks like the upper winds pushed us further north than we had thought. I've computed a course line to get us back on track soon, but we'll be eating into some of our reserve fuel. Jocko figures that we'll have only about two hours left by the time we reach Natal. And that's only if we lean out the fuel mixture to maintain best fuel consumption airspeed and if the upper winds don't mess us up again."

As soon as they reached the flight deck Ford examined the Mercator chart "You're sure about those star sights?"

"Yes, sir. The sky is clear and smooth. Those were three of the best fixes I've taken since leaving L.A."

"Then I guess we're just going to have to go with it. What's your best ETA at Natal?"

"I make it at right around 11:00 or 11:30 in the morning, Natal time."

Ford glanced at his watch. "Another eleven hours. And a two hour reserve from there gives us until about 1:30 P.M. to dry tanks." And here he paused. "We'd better damn well have a landfall by then. But I suggest we break out the emergency open-ocean landing procedures so that everyone can refresh himself on evacuation duties... just in case."

When Bob Ford suggested anything having to do with operational duties it was understood that such a 'suggestion' was tantamount to a direct order. All the crew members were soon immersed in the task of reviewing their respective duties in the event of a forced landing at sea. Everyone knew his assignment, but it was a drill that had to be constantly reviewed and kept fresh, if only in the back of their minds, as they went about the more normal routines of the flight.

Third Officer Jim Henricksen, taking his turn in the right cockpit seat, squinted through his sunglasses at the bright horizon ahead of him. The glare of the Equatorial sun was reflecting off the towering cumulus clouds just off the starboard bow, sending a flood of brilliant white light through the cockpit windscreen. It was 9 A.M. There was no sign of land. Christ, he thought to himself, I sure hope Brown's course correction was right. We ought to be sighting the coast by now. For all I know we could be just paralleling it on this heading. Wouldn't that be a crock: run out of gas with the coastline just over the horizon to the west. Damn it, I think we should take a more westerly heading...

'Land ho!" John Steers' shout grabbed everyone's attention.

"Where?"

"Dead abeam the port wing. About five miles. Looks like some sort of island." Steers announced, as he kept watch through the port cabin window just above the navigator's chart table.

Johnny Mack in the left cockpit seat, turned to look out his side window. Sure enough: they were just about to pass it. A small island... no... wait. Maybe we'd better check it out. Almost without thinking, Mack eased the big ship left to have a better look. "Hey, John check the chart. Can you get a fix on the name of that island? There seems to be two of them, one small one and then a bigger one south of it."

Steers reached for the South Atlantic chart which had been obtained from the British at Colombo. He scanned the area around the 'bulge' of Brazil where Natal was located. Sure enough, just northeast of Natal, about two hundred miles off the coast, there they were: two islands; one large, one smaller and what appeared to be a rock shoal west of them. No other prominent landmarks. "Bingo! They're the Fernando de Noronha Islands. Belong to Brazil, according to this map. Let's see..." he paused and took a plotting ruler and laid it on the map. "A heading of about 240 degrees and right around two hundred miles and we'll have Natal in our sights!"

The tensions of the long flight seemed to ease. All on the flight deck relaxed, glad in the knowledge that this longest leg of their journey was close to a safe conclusion.

"Jocko's Howgozit was right on the money." Swede Rothe announced from the engineer's station. "According to my fuel curve we ought to hit the water at Natal with just under two hours reserve. Hey, give that man a seegar!"

Bob Ford had been down below finishing breakfast when Johnny Mack swung the Boeing around to take a closer look at the islands. With his feel for every movement of the ship, he was well aware that something had changed. When he came up to the flight deck, Johnny Mack filled him in on the sighting and the seemingly pin-point accuracy of their navigation. "Good show, Johnny," Ford commented. "The rest ought to be a piece of cake. We're back in home territory from here on out."

Ford took his place in the left seat and Johnny Mack moved over to the right seat. The rest of the crew took care of their own duty rotations as they prepared for the landing at Natal. The long flight had given most of them an opportunity to take a reasonable amount of sleep during the night, so they were less fatigued than might have been expected. By the time Ford eased the big ship onto the water at Natal they had been in the air 23 hours and 35 minutes. When the Boeing was secured to the Pan American seaplane dock they all agreed to as short a stopover as possible. The finish line of their odyssey was in sight and they were eager to reach it.

CHAPTER XV
THE HOME STRETCH

The station manager of Pan American's Natal base smiled and extended his hand as Ford stepped onto the seaplane dock. "Welcome to Natal. We've been waiting for you. We received a dispatch from the U. S. Consulate office in town just a few hours ago. I guess you'll be happy to get this trip over with. Seems to me that you've had one hell of a long ride."

"Yeah, well, it's had its moments, I can tell you that. But speaking about getting it over with, what's the shortest turnaround time you can give us? My crew is really anxious to get going. We all managed to get a pretty good dose of shut-eye on this long leg from Leopoldville, so the sooner we can get out of here for Port-of-Spain, the better we'd all like it."

"The refueling should take a couple of hours, but there's one small hitch: we have some new health regulations now and we're required to spray every arriving aircraft for mosquitoes – they're trying to control an outbreak of yellow fever. We'll have to get all the crew off, send a spray crew on board and seal the aircraft for at least an hour while the insecticide does its job."

"That's new since I flew in here last. But, I guess we'll just have to put up with it. How about taking us all in for lunch while your people take care of that and the refueling. Then I'd like to plan a takeoff as soon as possible."

"Sure thing. Come on up to the office. I'll arrange for a crew bus to take all of you into town. Everything should be done by the time you get back."

When NC18602 had been properly secured the crew went ashore for lunch. Very shortly two men in protective rubber suits and masks, carrying portable spray tanks, went aboard. They closed and sealed the entry hatch behind them and proceeded to fill the Boeing with the fine mist of aerosol spray that would kill any errant mosquitoes that had hitched a ride from Africa. The men stayed aboard for almost an hour, and when the mist had settled, reappeared on the sea wing, hurriedly closed the entry hatch, and disappeared up the ramp and into a truck they had parked nearby earlier. Then they drove off hastily, in a cloud of dust, as if they were anxious to be somewhere other than on the Pan Am base.

About two hours later Ford and his crew were back from lunch. "Say," Ford remarked to the station manager, "ever since we left Khartoum we've had to put up with the damndest racket from Number One engine. The exhaust stack blew off and we've really not been able to repair it properly. Do you have anything in the way of a spare parts inventory that might include an exhaust stack we could use?"

The station manager thought a moment. "Not for that ship. You're the first B-314 that's ever come through here. I tell you what, though, we do have some spare parts we inherited from a wrecked PBY that came in here a while ago. If I'm not mistaken, they should include an exhaust stack. You want to check it out to see if it would fit? Maybe it could be rigged at least temporarily until you reach Port-of-Spain."

"I'll have Swede Rothe, my engineer, check it out. If anyone might figure a way to rig it, Swede sure could."

When Ford explained the situation to Rothe, the engineer shrugged. "Hell, we've gotten this far without it, but if you think it would do any good I'll take a look at it. Shouldn't be too much of a job to jury-rig it but I can't guarantee how long it would last."

"Well, do what you can. But let's try to wrap this up and get out of here as soon as possible."

Rothe and Jocko Parrish set to work trying to make the PBY stack fit the collector ring on the exhaust manifold. They managed to attach it, but the design differences made for some rather loose tolerances when it came to making it secure enough for the stresses of flight. Finally, they scrounged up some sheet metal, fashioned a reinforcing collar to fit around the whole assembly, and wired it in place with baling wire. Rothe stepped back and inspected their handiwork. "It ain't S-O-P[14] but maybe it'll hang together long enough to get us to our next stop."

An hour later the refueling was completed. Ford and the station manager walked down to the dock together as the rest of the crew went aboard. Ford remarked, "We'd better not delay any longer than we have to. The boys are really itching to get this whole affair over with, now that we're so close to home; and I'm damn certain the Company wants this bird back in the home nest pronto. The way they put it in that Plan A directive, it sounds as if they put a real high priority on putting these ships into some kind of support role as soon as possible."

The two stood silently for a moment, then Ford turned and extended his hand. "I guess it's time to go."

The station manager shook Ford's hand and nodded, "Get home safe."

Very quickly the four engines were started, the bow and tail lines released, and NC18602 moved out into the seaplane channel. Ford positioned the big ship midway between the left and right marker buoys that marked the beginning of the takeoff area, gave the signal to Swede Rothe, and moved the throttles forward to full takeoff power. The Boeing surged forward, spray flying. In a few seconds they were on the step and then airborne. Just at that moment, the jury-rigged exhaust stack blew off with a loud bang and once again the Number One engine started its incessant hammering noise.

"Well, so much for Yankee ingenuity!" Swede Rothe exclaimed. "That was sure a lot of damn wasted energy for nothing!"

"It was worth a try." Jocko Parrish tried to console him "You can't win 'em all, Swede."

Once at altitude, Ford turned the watch over to John Steers. As he stepped down from the left seat and walked toward the stairwell, Rod Brown, at the navigator's table, called him over.

"Yeah, Rod, what is it?"

"Skipper, I think something's fishy here. I know damn well that just before we went ashore for lunch I made certain to secure the ship's safe with all our receipts and papers. Just now I was going to add the Natal receipts to the list and when I went to open the safe, it was already unlocked. Somebody's been in there. All our receipts are gone. Along with some of the trip logs. If they'd been after money –

---

[14] S-O-P: Standard Operating Procedure

we sure didn't have any left. So why would they take the receipts and logs? They're not much good to anyone... unless it wasn't money they were after in the first place."

"What are you saying, Rod? That someone wanted our gas and food receipts and trip logs? The only thing I get from that is that someone was damned interested in where we've been."

"Yeah, and the best I can figure is it might have been those guys in the rubber suits. Could they have been spies?"

"It's possible. Brazil has a large immigrant population of both Germans and Japanese. Some of them might be spying for Japan or Germany. In any case, I don't know what we can do about it at this point. I suppose we could try to get a message to the station manager warning him about those guys if they show up again to spray other aircraft, but it would probably be a long-shot. If they were spies I don't think they'd hang around very long; especially if they think they got what they were looking for. Besides, any info they can get off those logs and receipts is probably stuff they already know anyway. We'll report it when we get to Port-of- Spain; but I wouldn't worry about it too much." With that, Ford went below to get his customary cup of coffee from the galley and Rod Brown turned back to the chart on the navigator's table.

On a course that roughly followed the Brazilian coastline, they flew past Fortaleza and entered the vast domain of the Amazon Basin. Late afternoon shadows created a mottled mosaic across the tops of the rain forest. The short-lived twilight soon gave way to the indigo of night. Once again they were flying as if enveloped in black velvet, except for the brilliant stars that spangled the upper hemisphere of sky. Soon, unseen by the crew, the city of Belem slipped abeam their wing and then they were crossing the great Amazon estuary. In this way they continued through the night; across the bulge of the Guianas and the northeast corner of Venezuela.

Thirteen hours after leaving Natal, Ford took over the left seat, eased the big Boeing down toward the harbor at Port-of-Spain, and with a smoothness born of long familiarity with the area, skimmed past the approach lights to the seaplane channel and settled the ship gently onto the water. It was 3 A.M. Altogether, they had been on the ship for more than forty hours since leaving Leopoldville.

Port-of-Spain was one of the more well-established of Pan American's South American bases. As soon as NC18602 was tied up to the seaplane dock, Ford alerted the chief ground mechanic

152

regarding the need to repair the Number One engine's exhaust stack. From their well-stocked store of spare parts, the local mechanics set to work fitting a new stack to the engine. Meanwhile, Ford and his crew boarded the crew limo and were taken to the local hotel where they all promptly bedded down and proceeded to sleep around the clock.

By noon on January 5th, most of the crew were pretty well slept out. With only one more flight leg left, they were eager to get going; to contact their families; to get back to as much of a normal routine as they could manage. The mood was expansive, relaxed, and upbeat as they gathered at the Pan American commissary for lunch.

"I sure hope the Company appreciates our efforts." John Steers remarked. "I'd say we've managed a lot more than just what you'd call 'above and beyond the call of duty'. I'll be damned if I ever want to see another bottle of English beer as long as I live! I can just picture that first case of Bud on ice that I'm going to order as soon as we hit New York. Mmmmmm!" and he half-closed his eyes in order to evoke that image.

"You can have your beer!" Swede Rothe chimed in. "I'm hopping the first plane for Oakland. When I come through that door at home the first two things I'm gonna do is drop my luggage and make love to my wife – not necessarily in that order!" he joked.

"Yeah, and I can finally get a decent change of clothes!" Jack Poindexter added. "At least you guys have had your regular two weeks worth of changes with you all the way. You know what it's like to have to live with yourself in the same set of underwear for six weeks?"

"We know! We know!" they all pinched their nostrils shut and pointed, laughing, at Poindexter.

"Yeah, but what now?" Eugene Leach interjected with a more serous note. "If the Company is turning over all our airplanes to the Navy, where does that leave us?"

"I'm willing to bet that we'll still be flying them," Ford replied, "but maybe under some kind of special service designation. Who knows, we could all be drafted into the Navy. Something like a merchant marine, except we'll be in airplanes instead of boats."

The rest of the lunch conversation centered on this still-unresolved issue of what was to happen to them after they arrived in New York. Pan American was well-known for its stiffly formal procedures in personnel matters. Unless you had a lot of seniority, you were pretty well at the mercy of the flight operations staffing board when it came to location and flight assignments. Now the factor of the war added a new uncertainty to the equation. In just a few more hours they would all have some answers to those questions.

By two in the afternoon the Port-of-Spain ground crews had completed the repairs to the Number One exhaust stack and the Clipper was fueled and stocked with provisions. Ford had contacted the operations supervisor earlier and now a new and up-to-date set of en route and approach and landing charts for the New York terminal were prominently laid out on the navigator's table. Refreshed and eager to be under way, they made short work of all pre-flight procedures. Within minutes, Ford had guided NC18602 to the departure end of the seaplane channel, turned around, and lined up for takeoff. "One more time, Swede..." Ford addressed his First Engineer. "Let's take it to the stops!"

Swede Rothe responded with a nod toward the cockpit and grasped the four throttle controls on the engineer's control panel. At the same time, Bob Ford took hold of the cockpit throttles and in unison they moved their respective controls smoothly against the full-power stops. Now, for the last time on this strange odyssey, the four Wright engines responded with the overpowering thunder of their combined 6000-plus horsepower and NC18602 surged forward with what seemed to be its own sense of eagerness. In seconds they were on the step, then airborne. They were into the final turn and the home stretch was finally in view.

Once again they flew through the afternoon and into the evening. Low clouds prevented them from sighting any of the islands of the West Indies as they proceeded on a direct course toward New York. Once darkness had fallen they all fell into the standard rotation of duties. But those whose turn it was to take some time off and relax in a bunk in the crew quarters, did not feel much like sleeping. The ship was charged with a sense of anticipation as each hour brought them closer to the end of their mission.

At 14 hours 45 minutes into the flight Bob Ford came up to the flight deck and took his place in the left seat. "Well, Johnny," he addressed his First Officer, "are you ready for this? We're about to rejoin the ranks of the workaday world!"

"Hey! I'm as ready as I'll ever be This has been one helluva Sunday drive. Let's do it!"

Bob Ford turned in his seat and called to Jack Poindexter at the radio desk. "Jack, I guess you can finally turn those radios on again. Get me a set-up on 2870 and pipe it up here. I'll make the first call for landing instructions."

Jack Poindexter gave a thumbs-up sign to his Captain. He flipped on the power switches for the transmitters and receivers, happy, at last, after many days of enforced inactivity, to be doing something useful. Once he had the terminal voice channel set up he switched it to the cockpit remote console and advised Ford that they were ready to transmit.

Bob Ford glanced at his wrist watch. 5:54 A.M. I guess it's time to give those LaGuardia boys a wake up call, he thought. He picked up his microphone, but paused with it poised just in front of his face. Just what the hell do you say after coming all this way? The simpler the better, I guess. Well, here goes. He pressed the microphone button with his thumb.

The morning was black and bitter cold. A mournful whisper of wind teased the outside of the glassed-in control tower. It was the only sound to be heard inside the dark interior where the lone mid-shift controller sat nursing his coffee mug. Aircraft movements during the night in the New York control area were minimal. His thoughts rambled. Two hours to go. God, I wish it was light already. Tough trying to stay awake on dull shifts like this when it stays dark so long. As soon as it's light I can at least pretend I'm not half asleep. Oh for that day shift next week...

"LAGUARDIA TOWER, LAGUARDIA TOWER – PAN AMERICAN CLIPPER NC18602, INBOUND FROM AUCKLAND, NEW ZEALAND. CAPTAIN FORD REPORTING. DUE TO ARRIVE PAN AMERICAN MARINE TERMINAL LAGUARDIA IN SEVEN MINUTES. OVER!"

"What the hell!"

Did he fall asleep and dream it? But in a couple of seconds he was fully alert and digested the full impact of the sudden presence blasting out of the loudspeaker. Hunching forward in his seat, he grabbed his microphone and, almost sub-consciously, out of long habit, responded. "PAN AMERICAN CLIPPER 18602. THIS IS LAGUARDIA TOWER, ROGER..." He paused.

"LaGuardia, this is Pan Am. D'ja hear that too? Sounds like we got us a surprise visitor." The second voice came over the intercom from Pan American's Flight Watch office at the Marine Terminal.

The tower controller reached for his intercom. "Yeah, uh, roger on that... What the hell are we supposed to do with him? He can't land in the seaplane channel in the dark. And where in hell did he pop up from anyway? We don't have any inbounds posted on the overseas board."

"I guess we just have to have him hold until daylight. Just hope he has enough gas."

"CLIPPER 18602, THIS IS LAGUARDIA. THE SEAPLANE CHANNEL IS CLOSED UNTIL DAYLIGHT. YOU WILL HAVE TO HOLD FOR ABOUT AN HOUR BEFORE WE CAN CLEAR YOU FOR LANDING. ADVISE INTENTIONS PLEASE."

"LAGUARDIA, ROGER, NO PROBLEM. WE CAN DO THAT."

"AND, SAY AGAIN, CONFIRM YOUR DEPARTURE POINT. WE SHOW NO OVERSEAS INBOUNDS AT THIS TIME."

"I SAY AGAIN, INBOUND FROM AUCKLAND, NEW ZEALAND, BY WAY OF THE LONG WAY 'ROUND FOR ABOUT THE PAST MONTH. IT'LL SURE BE GOOD TO GET HOME AGAIN."

The Pan Am flight watch operator who had intercepted the first inbound call promptly alerted Pan Am's Transatlantic Manager and the Public Relations Director. They, in turn, by a pre-arranged procedure, notified Army Intelligence and the Immigration Service. They all high-tailed their way to the airport. Except for these few, no one else was aware that history was about to be made.

As NC18602 came across the north shore of Long Island, Bob Ford peered through the blue-gray light of the cloudy dawn, seeking out the familiar landmarks that he knew would be there. Even though several years had passed since he had flown the Atlantic routes, his memory of the area was still clear. And the newly-acquired landing chart helped to pinpoint the necessary check points. Shortly he sighted the big natural gas tank on the Bronx shore, looming through the mist. Then he made out the familiar outline of the seaplane channel. Reducing power to a standard rate of descent, he gently brought the Boeing around toward the final approach path. With the relaxed familiarity of a man coming home, he eased into the final landing attitude. The touchdown was feather light. As the ship settled into its slow taxi mode, he glanced out his side window. The spray still splashing back over the sea wings was freezing into ice as it made contact with the metal surface. Sure looks cold out there. Hadn't thought about that. All this flying along the Equator I guess... forgot what winter is all about back here. Sure hope they have some warm jackets or blankets. Just then the Boeing took a strong lurch, skidded around to the right and came to a sudden stop. What the hell!

"Hey, Skipper," it was Johnny Mack, "I think we just got hung up on a sand bar."

"That wasn't supposed to be there, damn it! It's not marked on the landing chart as a posted obstruction. Thirty thousand miles of hell and we get snagged on a damned sandbar in New York!" Ford was generally regarded as a fairly even-tempered person. But this final obstacle to a successful end to their journey was the proverbial straw that broke the camel's back, and Ford's patience. Burning with pique, he slammed all four throttles to the full power stops. The sudden surge of full power tugged the big ship off the sandbar and once again into navigable water. Just as quickly, Ford brought the throttles back to normal taxi speed.

In short order they were moored to the docking buoy. As John Steers hung the hawser loop over the port bow stanchion he could see that it was encrusted with ice. He shivered in the unaccustomed chill of the bitter New York winter. It felt good to be home, but he could sure use some warm clothes right about now, he thought.

Following the crew debriefing in the operations office of Pan American's LaGuardia Marine Terminal, Bob Ford was asked to accompany the Army Air Force Intelligence team back to Washington where he was interviewed by the Chief of Naval Operations. They were mainly interested in whether or not he had any information regarding the whereabouts of certain U.S. Naval units with which they had lost contact in the confusing early days after Pearl Harbor. Ford informed them of his meeting with the PBY pilot in Surabaya and of the fate of the PBY squadron out of Cavite. He also mentioned their encounter with the Japanese submarine in the Bay of Bengal.

In its traditionally formal and precise way of handling personnel matters, Pan American allowed each crew member only two weeks leave before returning them to regular flight duties. Perhaps it was the urgency of the war; perhaps it was the war-time secrecy that inhibited them from making any public demonstration of appreciation for what they had accomplished. In any case, the only outward recognition consisted of a rather heavily-censored public relations announcement released to the press the day after they arrived at LaGuardia, and a small write-up in the next edition of the Pan Am house newsletter *New Horizons*.

Other Pan American Clippers and flight crews had also been caught out along the line on December 7th. They, too, had followed their 'Plan A' orders. But none had as far to go or as long to fly to return home safely as had the crew of NC18602. Several years into the post-war era, the records it had set would be eclipsed by the new generation of land-based commercial airliners. By then all the B-314s would be gone. Only the memories would remain, locked in the minds of Bob Ford and his crew. The stories told to their children and grandchildren would feed fertile imaginations as the epic flight became the stuff that legends are made of.

B-314 *Pacific Clipper's* (renamed from *California Clipper*) almost-around-the-world flight ends at LaGuardia Marine Air Terminal. The first secret U.S. war-related clipper mission out of New York to the Far East ("SM No.1") occurred just before the Pearl Harbor attack. Capt. R.O.D. Sullivan and a 16-man crew, without passengers were ordered on a 11,500-mile trek to Rangoon, Burma via Miami, San Juan, Belem, Natal, Dakar, Lagos, Leopoldville, Port Bell, Khartoum, Aden, Karachi, and Calcutta, carrying tons of ammo and weapons loaded at Miami for near-beleaguered American Volunteer Group forces in China fighting Japanese invasion troops. While using dead reckoning navigation in a heavy dust storm between Port Bell and Khartoum, Sullivan instinctively yanked the B-314 sharply to avoid striking a peaked mountain, the wing-on-end tilt of which spilled much of the stacked and bracketed cargo load.

NC18602 anchored in Bowery Bay upon completion of the historic flight, January 6, 1942.

POSTSCRIPT

The Crew

Captain Robert Ford

Following his arrival at LaGuardia and after the debriefing sessions, Bob Ford lost no time in taking a commercial flight back to San Francisco for a reunion with his wife, Betty. Following a welcome-home party with many of his friends, he returned to the routine of flight assignments across the Pacific.

Due to ill health, Bob resigned from Pan American in the summer of 1952. He and his wife moved from their small ranch in Martinez, California to a much larger ranch in the Mother Lode country north of Sacramento, California, where they raised cattle. Ranching was very successful in restoring his health but not at all profitable financially. With some reluctance he went back to flying in the mid-1950s.

Ford became a co-pilot in DC-4 freighters for Overseas National Airlines, flying between Oakland, California and Japan. He later became chief pilot, production flight test, for Lockheed Aircraft Service. There he and his crews test-flew Lockheed EC-121 and WV-3 radar picket planes after overhaul and before service acceptance by the Air Force or Navy. He later abandoned active flying to become Operations Engineer for the Flying Tiger Line, operating out of Burbank, California. He worked for them for several years and later served as a consultant for a few airline startup operations.

Ford returned to his ranch in the mid-1970s and spent the rest of his life ranching. He died there in 1994 at the age of 88.

1st Officer John Henry Mack

John Mack returned to regular flight duties with Pan Am. In the course of a 32 year career he became a Captain and flew the Pan Am routes throughout the world. Following the end of the flying boat era he flew DC-3s, Lockheed Constellations, Douglas DC-4s and DC7s, and Boeing 707s. He was captain of the first inaugural flight from the United States to London. He retired in 1972 and settled in Vacaville, California but continued to travel. One of his favorite places was Auckland, New Zealand, where he enjoyed fishing for marlin. He died in September, 1988.

Second Officer Roderick Norman Brown

According to excerpts from his flight logs, copies of which were provided to me by Mr. J. L. Johnson of Groton, CT, apparently, following the flight, Rod Brown was transferred to the Atlantic Division. He flew B314s on the routes out of New York to Miami, Port-of-Spain, Belem and Natal in Brazil, and on to Fisherman's Lake and Lagos in Africa. According to entries in his flight log, in May, 1942 he began trans-Atlantic flights between New York and Foynes, Ireland in the Vought-S44A aircraft. This would indicate that he left Pan American and went to work for American Export Airlines. Log entries as late as March, 1943 indicate that he remained with

American Export at least through that date. I have been unable to obtain any other information regarding his employment or whereabouts after that date other than that he died in 1972.

Fourth Officer John Delmer Steers

Upon arriving at LaGuardia, John Steers discovered that Pan American was transferring him to New York. He called his wife, Mary, who was still living in their new home in Palo Alto, California, and told her that she and their new son were going to have to move East. He remained there for a year and was then assigned to Miami. After five years, he was able to obtain a transfer to the Pacific Division. John and Mary returned to Palo Alto, and eventually settled in Los Altos Hills, California. He retired from Pan American in 1973. An avid aviation enthusiast, John owned and enjoyed light aircraft, and built his own *Stits Playboy* airplane. He also spent a good deal of time building race cars which featured innovative engineering designs, and many boats; especially a 50-foot fishing boat built with the assistance of two other Pan Am pilots. John died on December 30, 1994.

1st Flight Engineer Homans K. "Swede" Rothe

Swede returned to flight duty with the Pacific Division. Following his return to California he and his family made their home in the Delta country around Sacramento. He retired from Pan American in 1963. For several years they lived in Burney, California. He loved to go sailing, and for many years this was one of his major activities. Later they moved to Redding, California, where he died in 1992.

2nd Engineer John B. Parrish

"Jocko" Parrish continued flying for Pan Am and eventually became a Check Flight Engineer on the Boeing 707 based in San Francisco. In January, 1970 he checked out in the Boeing 747. Later that year he retired due to health problems and died in late 1970. This information is courtesy of former Pan Am Flight Engineers Pete Ryden and Tom Kewin and retired Pan Am 747 Captain Bobby George.

Chief Flight Radio Officer Jack Poindexter

Jack returned to his duties as Chief Flight Radio officer for the Pacific Division. He died sometime in the 1950s from cancer.

First Flight Radio Officer Oscar Hendrickson

Of all the crew members, Oscar Hendrickson had one of the more varied and colorful careers following the flight. Hendrickson was also transferred to the Atlantic Division. Six months later his first daughter, Barbara was born in New York City in 1942. After the war, he was reassigned to the Pacific Division on the "Orient Route". His second daughter, Katherine, was born in San Francisco in 1945. During 1946-47

Hendrickson was assigned to the Pan Am base at Midway Island as the resident radio engineer. He left Pan Am in 1953 and worked as a radio engineer for KSEN Radio in Shelby, Montana, and for KMON Radio in Great Falls.

During this period he also pursued his lifelong dream of becoming an attorney. He enrolled in the LaSalle Law Correspondence Course and studied for two years during his late night shifts at the KMON transmitter. In 1956, he sat for and passed the Montana Bar.

After a couple of years of private practice he ran and was elected to two terms as County Attorney for Blaine County from 1962 through 1970. During this time he prosecuted some local outlaws for cattle rustling. According to his daughter, Barbara, in the course of that investigation he was involved in some hair-raising chases on horseback that involved jumping across an irrigation ditch. The culmination of that chase and trial resulted in enough material that could have been used in an old-fashioned cowboy movie. Oscar was involved in his local community agendas for his entire tenure.

He was also a bit of a "cowboy". He had a horse and a truck. It was a Great Northern Railway truck with a flat bed that was 3 feet off the ground. All Oscar had to say was *GET IN THE TRUCK SKIDDO!!*" and the horse would leap three feet straight into the air - right up onto the flatbed. For many years he participated in the local parades exhibiting her unusual talent.

Oscar Hendrickson died on September 25, 1975, age 58. His wife, Grace, lived on to the age of 86. Today, his daughter Barbara Beeby lives in Helena Montana, and his daughter Katherine "Kitty" Tilleman lives with her husband in Chinook, Montana.

Radio Operator Eugene Leach

A few days after reaching LaGuardia, Eugene Leach was assigned as radio operator in charge of the Pan American radio station at Roberts Port, Liberia, on the west coast of Africa. He remained at this post for a year and a half. He was then transferred to the Pacific Division and assigned as operator in charge of the Pan American radio station at Pearl City, Hawaii. He held that post for one year. Then he was assigned to flight duty based out of San Francisco. In 1946 Eugene resigned from Pan American to go to work for his father in a Ford dealership in East Oakland, California. He held this job until 1959, then moved to San Ramon, California, where he opened an A & W Root Beer franchise. He ran this business until he retired in 1980. Eugene Leach died at his home in San Ramon in April, 2000.

Flight Steward Barney Sawicki	Assistant Flight Steward Verne C. Edwards

Both are deceased, but I have no other information as to their activities or whereabouts after the flight.

3rd Officer James G. Henricksen

I have been unable to locate any information regarding the activities or whereabouts of Jim Henricksen after the flight.

The Mechanics

Verne White, Bud Washer, and Ralph Hitchcock were eventually picked up from their foreign assignments and returned to the United States. I do not have information as to their specific work assignments after returning home. Verne White died in April, 2001 and Ralph Hitchcock died on October 13, 2006.

The Aircraft

After a thorough inspection by Pan American mechanics, NC18602 was assigned to service with the Atlantic Division. It remained there until May, 1943 when it was returned to the Pacific Division. It continued in service through the final months of the Naval Air Transport contract and, for a short time after the war, under the renewed civilian operation until it was rendered obsolete by the coming of the faster, more efficient land planes of the post-war period. Its final fate is unknown; but, most likely, as with most of Pan Am's flying boats, it was declared surplus by the War Assets Administration and sold for scrap.

A full-scale model of a Boeing B314 flying boat is on display at the Foynes Flying Boat Museum at Foynes, Ireland. For more information about this model and the museum go to www.flyingboatmuseum.com. Photo by Ed Dover

Ed Dover seated at his old radio operator station on flight deck of the B314 model at Foynes, 2007. Photo by Ed Dover

166

APPENDIX
THE DELAY IN KHARTOUM

Shortly before we went to press with the original manuscript, Mr. Douglas Miller of Pelican Films, provided a copy of a hand-written letter which he had found in a collection of papers loaned to him by Betty Ford. The letter, dated 29 December 1941, and mailed at Cairo, was on Pan American Airways System letterhead and signed by a "Jim Smith." It requested Captain Ford to wait at Khartoum for priority passengers and cargo. Smith must have been a Pan American employee, but his official position is not indicated. The text of that letter follows:

Cairo
Dec 29th
11 pm
Dear Bob,

The news of your arrival in Khartoum has just reached here and I have been asked by General Adler, Commanding U.S. Military Mission in Near East to have you wait in Khartoum until Wednesday night or Thursday morning to take a load of official mail & passengers to the U.S. I do not know what your orders are, from whom they came or if you would have space from Khartoum to U.S. The situation here is that Cairo has been cut off so far as communications are concerned from the U.S. and you are the best chance of getting important military information to Washington that will probably come up for some time.

A radio has already been sent you from Middle East Command R.A.F. about this or at least about your plans for return to U.S. You may not receive this as the radio is damn slow due to coding. If you do not have it before this, please send us by urgent radio – ask AOC Khartoum to send this "signal" through "Headquarters Middle East to General Adler." Rammer will tell you how to handle it – the following information:

1) How many pounds of additional load could you take to U.S.?

2) What is last day on which you can leave Khartoum (This and next question is only important if you have space available.)

3) If you must leave Khart. (sic) at once is your itinerary such that passengers & mail leaving here Wednesday could overtake you at Lagos – i.e., cargo would leave here Wed, leave Khartoum Thursday, leave Maiduguri Friday and be at Lagos Friday night.

In conclusion General Adler considers it very important that you wait at Khart or Lagos if you have any space available and I feel you should do it unless you have orders to proceed at once from authority at least equal to General Adler. We are now making arrangements for special plane to leave here Wednesday so you may be assured that it will arrive Khart Wednesday night.

In haste,
Good luck & Regards
Jim Smith

I do not know if Bob Ford ever received this letter. It is evident from the information in John Steers' log and from my interviews with Captain Ford that they considered the delay at Khartoum the result of bureaucratic fumbling rather than a priority issue involving important war information. Neither of them make any mention of a letter from Cairo. In any case, they were not planning on stopping at Lagos. Furthermore, the amount of fuel they would have to carry, plus the weight of the remaining spare engine parts still on board, would have put the ship so far over gross weight that it would have been impractical to take on any additional cargo or passengers between Leopoldville and Natal. I can only assume, at this late date, that Ford did transport the one woman passenger from Khartoum to Leopoldville, but from there on they were unable to comply fully with the request from Cairo.

BIBLIOGRAPHY AND SOURCE MATERIALS

Bibliography

Daley, Robert, *An American Saga,* Random House, New York, 1980, pp. 323-329.

Cohen, Stan, *Wings to the Orient,* Pan American Clipper Planes 1935 to 1945, Pictorial Histories Publishing Company, Missoula, Montana, 1985.

Gandt, Robert L., *China Clipper, The Age of the Great Flying Boats,* Naval institute Press, Annapolis, Maryland, 1991.

Lester, Valerie, *Fasten Your Seat Belts!,* Paladwr Press, McLean, Virginia, 1995, pp. 20-27.

Pan American Airways, *New Horizons,* in-house company magazine, January 1942, pp. 11-13, somewhat censored article describing the flight of NC18602.

Albert S. J. Tucker, Jr. and Matthew W. Paxton IV with Eugene Dunning, *Pacific Clipper – The Untold Story,* The News-Gazette Print Shop, 109 S. Jefferson Street, Lexington, Virginia, 2001

Prange, Gordon W*., At Dawn We Slept – The Untold Story of Pearl Harbor*, McGraw-Hill Books, New York, 1981,   p. 387

Beall, Wellwood E., Engineer-in-charge – Boeing Aircraft Company, *Design Aspects of the Boeing Trans-Atlantic Clipper,* a technical paper presented to the Air Transport Meeting of the Institute of Aeronautical Sciences at Chicago, November 18 and 19, 1938. (Photo-copy of this paper provided by Boeing Aircraft Company).

Boeing Aircraft Company, *Boeing Model 314 Transoceanic Clipper,* a brochure describing the technical and operational features of the B314. (Photo-copy of this brochure provided by Boeing Aircraft Company).

New York Times, January 7 1942, article, *Pacific Clipper, Racing War, Circles Globe, Lands Here,* by Byron Darton. Also a somewhat censored article describing the flight of NC18602.

Vacaville Reporter, VISTA Magazine, January, 1972, pp. 11-13, *Thirty-Two Years in the Wild Blue: The Global Odyssey of a Pilot,* by Jim Jones.

Personal Sources

My first hand experience was flying aboard Pan American Clippers between 1942 and 1948 as a flight radio officer. This included several flights on NC18602 between San Francisco and Honolulu. I was a ground station operator at the Pearl City base and at Noumea, New Caledonia, during the period 1943-1944.

In January, 1992 I visited Captain Ford at his ranch in Northern California and spent two days as his guest, obtaining several hours of taped interviews. He gave me a copy of the flight log kept by Fourth Officer John D. Steers.

In August, 1993 I visited Eugene Leach, the radio operator who came on board NC18602 at Noumea. He gave me additional photo-copies of John Steer's flight log. During this same trip I re-visited Captain Ford and stayed overnight as his guest. During that time we reviewed the information obtained from the first interview. In October 1997 I had several telephone conversations with Eugene

Leach at which time he was able to clarify certain points in the narrative.

During August 1996 and most recently in July, 2009 I corresponded with J. L. Johnson, Jr. of Groton, Connecticut. Mr. Johnson has researched the history of Pan American Airways flights for a number of years. He provided me with a copy of a report he received regarding the naming of Clipper aircraft, and copies of articles reporting on Captain Ford's flight from the February 1942 issue of <u>The Bee Hive</u>, the in-house company magazine of United Aircraft Corporation. In July, 2009 he sent me copies of pages from 2nd Flight Officer Rod Brown's flight log. Brown's entries confirm the use of two B314s during the flight.

Details of some of the biographical sketches included in the Postscript were obtained from: Betty Ford, wife of Captain Robert Ford; Mary Steers, wife of Fourth Officer John Steers; Marian Rothe, wife of First Engineering Officer Swede Rothe; Barbara Beery and Katherine "Kitty" Tilleman, daughters of Flight Radio Officer Oscar Hendrickson; and Eugene Leach, the extra radio operator taken on board at Noumea.

During the course of writing this story, wherever I found a discrepancy between bibliography sources and my personal sources, I chose to use the information from my personal sources; particularly certain details of the flight as related to me directly by Captain Ford.

Ed Dover and wife Nancy at the Pan Am Clipper docking site at Pearl City in 2006. The memorial plaque was placed there on November 22, 1985 by employees of Pan American celebrating the 50th anniversary of Trans-Pacific flight. Photo by Ed Dover.

Made in the USA
Middletown, DE
05 May 2024

53896457R10106